# UNDERSTANDING

# REASONABLE

# FORCE

## MARK DAWES

The Derwent Press
Derbyshire, England

www.derwentpress.com

# UNDERSTANDING REASONABLE FORCE
## By Mark Dawes

## All Rights Reserved.

## Copyright NFPS Ltd 2006

ISBN 1-84667-012-8

Cover Photograph:
Martin Lewis
www.martinlewis.biz

Cover design and book design by:
Pam Marin-Kingsley
www.far-angel.com

**Published in 2006 by
The Derwent Press
Derbyshire, England
www.derwentpress.com**

This book is dedicated to my wife, Deborah, my rock and bulwark, whose support, tolerance, forgiving nature and continual inspiration has made me a better man than I ever thought possible. It is also dedicated to my children, Katie and Billy, our family's psychologists and philosophers, who provide me with my purpose and direction in life and who teach me more about human behaviour and the beauty and quality of life than any philosopher could. They are good kids and a credit to us both.

I would also like to dedicate this book to my closest friend and mentor, John Steadman, whose influence on my physical capability has been like the opening of a door, before which I was only peering through a keyhole. His integrity and passion make him a king among men. We are brothers bonded by the flames of the past and cast as family in stone.

Finally I would like to dedicate this book to my brother, Colin, who was sadly taken from us at the premature age of 56 last year. He has been with me at every major event of my life and I miss him dearly. His passion for life was infectious, and his sense of humour and gift for living always brought a ray of sunshine into all of our lives. His untimely passing served to re-enforce the fact that life is too short—we should all never take tomorrow for granted, but live each day fully with the aim of making each day take us one step closer to becoming the better person we all know we can be.

# Contents

.

# Introduction

The basis for this book is our on-going research and development in the field of personal safety and physical skills training that raised questions which we needed to find answers to thus helping us to better understand the rights and responsibilities of individuals so that we may better instruct them in a more competent manner.

My need to understand the complexities of reasonable force has been a continual driving motivation for me ever since I started teaching, and one that has been fuelled by my initial lack of understanding of the law and also my disdain for some of the advice that was given to me on the subject which I couldn't understand at the time.

My aim in writing this book is that I hope it will provide answers to many questions that you, like myself, have been asking over the years in the hope of improving our professional competence, in a language we both understand.

Understanding what we can and cannot do with regard to our rights (and responsibilities) in relation to the use of 'reasonable force' is not just about learning physical skills. It is about understanding the rights and responsibilities of each and every one of us as individuals within the framework of what the law allows and prohibits. The law is as important, if not more important, than physical technique as it will always be the application of the use of force within the circumstances and the resultant harm caused or prevented as a result of the use of force that will be judged, not the technique used. Thereby, be wary of people who tell you that they can teach you *"legally correct techniques"* as no such technique exists.

As a citizen of the UK my hope is that this book will improve your self-worth and self-confidence by allowing you to understand your rights and responsibilities in relation to the use of reasonable force more clearly.

If you are a personal safety or self-defence instructor reading this book my hope is that it will assist you in allowing you to give your students and clients practical advice based on the principles of the law in relation to reasonable force. The scope of this book is intended to cover the use of reasonable force in its broad sense, and will draw reference from case studies and give examples where necessary to clarify the points made.

Please note however that this book is not intended to be used as a legal document, and has not been written by a lawyer. We have however taken as much due diligence as we can to ensure that what is written here is as accurate as it can be based on our own personal knowledge and experience at the time of writing it. To this extent our work has been subject to a legal audit by a Barrister at Law (CBE). In addition our training is continually monitored as part of our ongoing quality management system in line with current health and safety legislation to ensure that we continually strive to improve our understanding and professional competence to the best of our knowledge and ability.

# About the author, Mark Dawes

## Qualifications:

- Awarded Diploma of Senior Tutor Trainer with Recognised status as National Coach Tutor for Occupational Physical Restraint/ Intervention and Disengagement Physical Skills Training, including Train the Trainer Development Programmes.
- Awarded National Ratification Officer Status.
- Qualified Stress Consultant
- Associate Member of IOSH (Institute of Occupational Safety & Health)
- Licensed Master Practitioner of Neuro-Linguistic Programming
- Qualified TFT Practitioner
- Registered on the list of Experts held by the Expert Witness Institute

# Mark Dawes

Mark is Director & National Coach Tutor of NFPS Ltd, an organisation that specializes in conflict management and occupational physical skills training (physical restraint and self-defence/breakaway).

He has worked as a prison officer and hostage negotiator and is a competent physical skills instructor with over twenty-eight years of experience.

As an Expert Witness he provides reports and testimony for Court and was recently engaged as an Expert Witness for the defence in a Manslaughter case involving the death of a person during restraint in which the defendants were found not guilty.

He holds the awards of National Coach Tutor and National Ratification Officer awarded to him by the British Ju-Jitsu Governing Body, an independent body registered with Sport England and the Central Council for Physical Education, for the development, delivery, accreditation and ratification of all Occupational Physical Intervention and Disengagement Physical Skills Training, including Train the Trainer Development Programmes.

Mark is also a Licensed Master Practitioner of NLP (Neuro-Linguistic Programming). Licensed and certified by The Society of Neuro-Linguistic Programming founded by Dr. Richard Bandler—the co-founder of NLP. He was trained by Richard

Bandler, Paul McKenna, John La Valle and Michael Neill, leading authorities of NLP in the World today.

His training incorporates and positively embraces NLP philosophy and attitude in its consultative and training structure to enable for effective change to take place.

He has been constructing and delivering training programmes in the field of Personal Safety and Conflict Management since 1988, and was the Personal Safety Advisor to the Hillingdon Crime Prevention Panel for over 5 years working in liaison with the local Metropolitan Police Crime Prevention Officers running personal safety courses in the West London Area.

As a Consultant Trainer over the years he has also provided training to many thousands of individuals including: Social Services staff, Courtroom staff, Local Authority staff, Healthcare staff, Transport companies, Pharmaceutical companies, Security organisations and Military personnel.

During Mark's professional career he has worked in partnership with his clients to provide them with occupational specific training packages to address the risks that their staff encounter. To this end, he can support his training with policy and procedural documentation and risk assessments to help reduce the liability of staff and their employer.

In the retail industry he has constructed and delivered courses for such organisations as Safeway and Capper & Co (a Spar organisation). All courses are fully risk-assessed and Mark has undertaken a number of specific retail surveys and reports which have provided him with the knowledge to devise training courses, policies and procedures to meet the specific needs of his clients whilst reducing the liability of the organisation and their staff.

The training and consultancy provided by Mark complies with all of the relevant statute (including the Human Rights Act 1998 and the Health and Safety at Work Act and associated Regulations). Mark Dawes also undertakes ongoing legal training in civil and criminal law and has had all of this training audited for legal accuracy by a Barrister at Law and former Member of Parliament who was awarded the CBE.

# Understanding Reasonable Force

# Chapter I
# How it All Started.

*"To understand the battle you must know the language."*

—The Language of Combat

Many years ago, in 1988 to be precise, I was approached by the local Metropolitan Police to assist in the running of some self-defence and personal safety courses for the local Crime Prevention Panel. Apparently it seemed that the Police had decided not to run any further physical self-defence courses for non-police staff due to lack of insurance cover.

At the time I was running martial arts classes at a local sports centre so I was pretty up on technique (at least that's what I thought), but not so up on the law or any form of preventative measures for that fact—apart from telling people that the best form of defence was to run away (the old 'get out of jail free card' advice from instructors, who like me at the time, had no real working knowledge of the law or personal safety).

Anyway, as a result of that meeting and subsequent meetings with the local Police and various Crime Prevention Panel volunteers, it was decided that we should run our first course. It was at the DHL offices in West London and I was teamed up with a Police trainer. The course was to run for two hours, one day a week over a six-week period, and to take place after work between 5.30 – 7.30 in the evening. My role was to do the physical bit (the bit the Police couldn't do) and the Police Officer was there to give personal safety advice and answer any questions in relation to 'reasonable force' (the bit that I couldn't do).

The course seemed to be going to plan. We had done the introductions and had started on the first physical session. The women (the course only consisted of women—no men attended—no surprise there) were enjoying the physical bit and we felt that we were onto a good thing and that the partnership was working.

After a while we decided to have our first break and, on return, the Police Officer gave them a lecture on personal safety focusing on preventative strategies that they could adopt to make them less likely to become victims in the first place. He showed a short video, and then he gave a 20-minute talk on how and what they could do to avoid the likelihood of being 'targeted' by opportunist criminals. The lecture seemed to go down well and everything was going to plan.

# Understanding Reasonable Force

That done we got up and continued with the physical bit for about another 30 minutes which everyone was enjoying.

At the end of that session we had about 20-30 minutes left which we had set aside for a course wash-up and de-brief and for questions and answers. Once all the women had sat down, the Police Officer again took over as planned and asked if they had enjoyed themselves to which we received a resounding, 'YES!', which made us feel really good (a bit of an ego massage going on I suppose). Then he asked if any of them had any questions about the training or anything else that they would like to know about, and that's when it started to happen.

This was the turning point that set my definitive purpose for the rest of my life up to this point, and one which has led me to write this book.

A lady sat in the middle row raised her hand.

'Yes', said the Police Officer. "What would you like to know?'

'Well', said the woman. 'We have heard you talk about reasonable force today and that we have the right to use it if attacked'.

'That's correct', said the Police Officer. 'You do have that right, and no-one can take it away from you as that is the law'.

'*That's all well and good*', said the woman. '*But would you mind explaining to me what reasonable force actually means as I'm not sure I understand it fully*'.

As she asked the question I could see quite a few other women look at each other and nod their heads in apparent agreement with her question.

'*Of course*', said the Police Officer, and he proceeded to give the following explanation which has stayed with me ever since: '*Reasonable force is a common law right and also a statute right contained in section 3(1) of The Criminal Law Act 1967 which gives you, and all other citizens, the right to use reasonable force in defence of yourself, and/or others, and to protect your property and to prevent a crime. However, "reasonable force" is not defined by the Act and the only people who can tell you whether or not the force you used was reasonable or not will be a magistrate or a jury, dependent on where you are tried. Therefore, if you use force and you are charged with assault, but the magistrate or jury find that the force you used was reasonable, you will be found not guilty of the charge of assault. However, if they find that the force you used was unreasonable, or excessive, then you may be found guilty of assault and sentenced accordingly*'.

'*Sorry*', said the woman. '*Either I've missed something here or you haven't answered my question. I want to know what "Reasonable Force" means otherwise how will I know what would be considered "reasonable" or "unreasonable and excessive"?*'

# Understanding Reasonable Force

I was also starting to become confused at the advice being given and I must admit I was praying silently that no-one would ask me for my opinion as I hadn't a clue as to what reasonable force meant, and to be honest, the Police Officer's response had confused me even further.

Again (thankfully) the Police Officer tried to answer the question by basically repeating what he had previously said, but by also adding: *'Each situation has to be judged on its own individual circumstances, and as each situation will be different no-one can provide a specific example of what would be reasonable as it will depend entirely on the circumstances in which the force was used'*.

However, again the woman replied that he still hadn't answered her question. At this stage, the other women were now joining in the debate wanting to know more specifically what reasonable force meant.

One woman said: *'Are you saying that we have to judge what force would be reasonable in a given situation dependent on all of the circumstances?'*

*'Yes'*, said the Police Officer. *'That's exactly what I'm saying'*.

*'Then wouldn't it be useful for us to know what "reasonable" means, don't you think?'* said the woman.

Then another woman joined in: *'I'm having enough trouble remembering the techniques that I was taught an hour ago. If I'm being attacked how am I supposed to be expected to think about everything that's going on and then try to remember what technique would be best?'*

The Police Officer gave the standard "off-the-shelf" answer; *'That's why you need to train regularly'*, he said.

Then came the crunch. Having given up on the Police Officer the woman who asked the initial question then posed her question to me.

*'Can you tell me what it means?'* she said.

I felt my mouth go dry and my rear-end grip the seat that I wanted to disappear into as the entire group turned their attention onto me. Even the Police Officer was looking at me with an expression that seemed to convey that he was hoping that I would come out with something that would get us out of the hole we had found ourselves in.

Luckily, I had learned one thing from my days in the Royal Navy which had always stood me in good stead and this was 'If you don't know the answer be honest and say so. Don't attempt to waffle your way out of it but say that you will find out.' So that's exactly what I did.

# Understanding Reasonable Force

I said: *'I'm sorry I don't know what it means. I'm here to teach the physical techniques and the Police are here to answer those sorts of questions as they have the knowledge in that area. However, I promise you that by the next lesson next week I'll have a better answer for you'.*

That seemed to satisfy and placate the group for the moment and got us temporarily out of the hole, at least until the next week's lesson.

As the women started to file out of the room at the end of the first evening, the Police Officer, who I'd been working with, turned to me and said, *'I'm looking forward to next week. It normally takes five years to get a law degree and you're going to do it in seven days. Good luck!'*

In short, I had seven days to provide a better answer than my Police Officer colleague had and I had promised I do it.

That was the start of my journey. I was on a mission to find out what reasonable force meant so that I would never be placed in a situation again whereby I couldn't answer a question fully and with conviction. I was also very conscious at first of the fact that I was not a lawyer and I didn't have a law degree. Therefore, I was unsure of whether or not I would be allowed to give advice on reasonable force—or more importantly, whether I would get into trouble for doing it if I did. I even thought about taking a law degree, but I didn't want to. The reason was that I didn't want to practice law as a lawyer, and I couldn't see the point of having to study the whole aspect of law required for a degree to learn about one area of it. And this is something you can learn right now, you do not have to be a lawyer to express an opinion about the law, and you have the right to impart information and ideas to anyone you wish.

This right is even enshrined by *Article 19* of *The Universal Declaration of Human Rights* which states:

*"Everyone has the right to freedom of opinion and expression; this right includes freedom to hold opinions without interference and to seek, receive and impart information and ideas through any media and regardless of frontiers."*

However, what I would suggest to you is make sure that you are confident that what you are saying is right. You won't gain the credibility you need by not going that extra mile. I was fortunate enough to have the help of a number of people who have guided me through the complexities of this area of law. Some were solicitors and barristers and some were not. Some of the best help I have had is from people who still send me newspaper clippings or articles by e-mail or in the post. So, if you want to know more, ask people to help you and you may be surprised how many will. For me, the quest seemed simple. If I have the right to use reasonable force I want to be able to know what that right means, and also, possibly more importantly, what the restrictions are that are also imposed by having such a right.

# Understanding Reasonable Force

More importantly for me however, was that I wanted to be able to tell people about that right in a language that they could understand, as best as I can, by replacing the legal 'jargon' with more everyday words used by everyday people.

To date I must be doing something right as I am now one of the few Expert Witnesses on the subject and I have been used to advise solicitors and barristers on my area of expertise by providing a more holistic approach to the subject by combining my self-study on the law with my study of health and safety, human factors and coaching knowledge.

To be able do this, I first had to believe that I could do it, and when I had my moments of doubt, as we all do, I always remembered the words of a man who was once a small, black dyslexic boy whose mission in wanting to learn to fight was so that he could beat up the person who stole his bike. That man is Muhammad Ali, who in my opinion is not only possibly the greatest boxer that ever lived, but also a great philosopher and humanitarian. He said:

*"I know where I'm going and I know the truth and I don't have to be what you want me to be. I'm free to be what I want".*

I also draw reference to Nelson Mandela who quoted Marianne Williamson in his inaugural speech, 1994:

*"Our deepest fear is not that we are inadequate. Our deepest fear is that we are powerful beyond measure. It is our light, not our darkness, that most frightens us. We ask ourselves, who am I to be brilliant, successful, talented and fabulous? Actually, who are you NOT to be? You are a child of God. Your playing small doesn't serve the world. There's nothing enlightened about shrinking so that other people won't feel insecure around you. We were born to make manifest the glory that is within us. It's not just in some of us; it's in EVERYONE! And as we let our own light shine, we unconsciously give other people permission to do the same. As we are liberated from our own fear, our presence automatically liberates others!"*

What you will read now is a culmination of the work that has been put into getting to where I have got to today with regard to my understanding of reasonable force.

I sincerely hope that you find this book not only an enjoyable read but also an educational journey helping you to develop your understanding of this area of law in a way that is easy to read and reference.

# Chapter 2
# A Historical Review of the Law in Relation to Reasonable Force

*"Injustice anywhere is a threat to justice every-where"*.

—Martin Luther King (1963)

## The case of Tony Martin

The case of the Norfolk farmer, Tony Martin, prompted a fierce debate on the law with regard to a person's right to defend themselves, and in particular, the issue of what constitutes *"reasonable force"*.

The judge at the trial of Tony Martin, jailed for the killing of Fred Barras, Mr Justice Owen, told the jury:

*'You have to try to ascertain what was in Mr Martin's mind at the time—what circumstances did he believe he was facing? He has said he believed he might be attacked. Was it reasonable? Should he have shouted out, should he have fired one shot, and so on?'*

22

*The Criminal Law Act 1967* states that if only reasonable force has been used, no crime has been committed and the defendant must go free. If, as in a case such as Tony Martin's, where the burglar is killed, and the jury decides the level of force was unreasonable, the jurors must then decide whether the force used amounts to murder. To be convicted of murder, the defendant need not have intended to kill. It has only to be established that he intended to cause serious harm.

In the case of Tony Martin, the jury appeared to have accepted the prosecution's case that Mr Martin fired not in self-defence but "in accordance with his views that the only way to stop thieves was to shoot them". The prosecution argued that Mr Martin intended "to kill or cause really serious injury". The case of Mr Martin echo's a similar case of a Captain Moir, a man who held too rigid an idea of his authority in law which will be looked at later on in this book.

However, under the broad interpretation of *'reasonable force'* there are occasions where lethal force can be used and where pre-emptive strikes can be regarded as necessary.

One of the first people to address the doctrine of self-defence was A.V.Dicey[1].

---

[1] From A.V. Dicey; "The Law of the Constitution" Macmillan, London, 1885, (Eighth Edition, 1915) - Note IV, The Right of Self-Defence, pp.489-97.

# Understanding Reasonable Force

Albert Venn Dicey (1835-1922) was amongst the first academics at London School of Economics, lecturing from 1896-99 and contributing to the School's intellectual development in its formative years.

Called to the Bar in 1863, Dicey had combined a legal career with political journalism during the 1860s and 1870s before his appointment to the Vinerian Chair of English Law at Oxford in 1882. Dicey's reputation rested upon his academic quality. *The Law of the Constitution*, published in 1885, made his name (Gladstone described it in Parliament as a recognised authority), and his scholarly work was cited in Parliament in the Irish Home Rule question during the 1880s.

The following is an extract from A.V. Dicey; "The Law of the Constitution" Macmillan, London, 1885, (Eighth Edition, 1915). This extract has had a major impact on the way the defence of self-defence is raised and judged in English law and as such provides an excellent background and historical reference to the principles that hold true today.

How far has an individual a right to defend his person, liberty, or property, against unlawful violence by force, or [if we use the word "self-defence" in a wider sense than that usually assigned to it] what are the principles which, under English law, govern the right of self-defence?

The answer to this inquiry is confessedly obscure and indefinite, and does not admit of being given with dogmatic certainty; nor need this uncertainty excite surprise, for the rule which fixes the limit to the right of self-help must, from the nature of things, be a compromise between the necessity, on the one hand, of allowing every citizen to maintain his rights against wrongdoers, and the necessity, on the other hand, of suppressing private warfare. Discourage self-help, and loyal subjects become the slaves of ruffians. Over-stimulate self-assertion, and for the arbitrament of the Courts you substitute the decision of the sword or the revolver.

Let it further be remarked that the right of natural self-defence, even when it is recognised by the law, does not imply "a right of attacking", for instead of attacking one another for injuries past or impending, men need only have recourse to the "proper tribunals of justice."

A notion is current, for which some justification may be found in the loose dicta of lawyers, or the vague language of legal text-books, that a man may lawfully use any amount of force which is necessary, and not more than necessary, for the protection of his legal rights. This notion, however popular, is erroneous. If pushed to its fair consequences, it would at times justify the shooting of trespassers, and would make it legal for a schoolboy, say of nine years old, to stab a hulking bully of eighteen who attempted to pull the child's ears.

# Understanding Reasonable Force

Some seventy years ago or more a worthy Captain Moir carried this doctrine out in practice to its extreme logical results. His grounds were constantly infested by trespassers. He gave notice that he should fire at any wrongdoer who persisted in the offence. He executed his threat, and, after fair warning, shot a trespasser in the arm. The wounded lad was carefully nursed at the Captain's expense. He unexpectedly died of the wound. The Captain was put on his trial for murder; he was convicted by the jury, sentenced by the judge, and, on the following Monday, hanged by the hangman. He was, it would seem, a well-meaning man, imbued with too rigid an idea of authority.

He perished from ignorance of law. His fate is a warning to theorists who incline to the legal heresy that every right may lawfully be defended by the force necessary for its assertion.

The maintainable theories as to the legitimate use of force necessary for the protection or assertion of a man's rights, or in other words the possible answers to our inquiry, are, it will be found, two, and two only.

## The First Theory.

In defence of a man's liberty, person, or property, he may lawfully use any amount of force which is both "necessary"—i.e. not more than enough to attain its object—and "reasonable" or "proportionate"—i.e. which does not inflict upon the wrongdoer mischief out of proportion to the injury or mischief which the force used is intended to prevent; and no man may use in defending his rights an amount of force which is either unnecessary or unreasonable. This doctrine of the "legitimacy of necessary and reasonable force" is adopted by the Criminal Code Bill Commissioners. It had better be given in their own words:

"We take [they write] one great principle of the common law to be, that though it sanctions the defence of a man's person, liberty, and property against illegal violence, and permits the use of force to prevent crimes, to preserve the public peace, and to bring offenders to justice, yet all this is subject to the restriction that the force used is necessary; that is, that the mischief sought to be prevented could not be prevented by less violent means; and that the mischief done by, or which might reasonably be anticipated from the force used is not disproportioned to the injury or mischief which it is intended to prevent. This last principle will explain and justify many of our suggestions. It does not seem to have been universally admitted; and we have therefore thought it advisable to give our reasons for thinking that it not only ought to be recognised as the law in future, but that it is the law at present."

The use of the word "necessary" is, it should be noted somewhat peculiar, since it includes the idea both of necessity and of reasonableness. When this is taken into account, the Commissioners' view is, it is submitted, as already stated, that a man may lawfully use in defence of his rights such an amount of force as is needful for their protection and as such, does not inflict, or run the risk of inflicting, damage out of all proportion to the injury to be averted, or (if we look at the same thing from the other side) to the value of the right to be protected. This doctrine is eminently rational. It comes to us recommended by the high authority of four most distinguished judges. It certainly represents the principle towards which the law of England tends to approximate. But there is at least some ground for the suggestion that a second and simpler view more accurately represents the result of our authorities.

## The Second Theory.

A man, in repelling an unlawful attack upon his person or liberty, is justified in using against his assailant so much force, even amounting to the infliction of death, as is necessary for repelling the attack—i.e. as is needed for self-defence; but the infliction upon a wrongdoer of grievous bodily harm, or death, is justified, speaking generally, only by the necessities of self-defence—i.e. the defence of life, limb, or permanent liberty.

This theory may be designated as the doctrine of "the legitimacy of force necessary for self-defence." Its essence is that the right to inflict grievous bodily harm or death upon a wrongdoer originates in, and is limited by, the right of every loyal subject to use the means necessary for averting serious danger to life or limb, and serious interference with his personal liberty.

The doctrine of the "legitimacy of necessary and reasonable force" and the doctrine of the "legitimacy of force necessary for self-defence" conduct in the main, and in most instances, to the same practical results.

On either theory A, when assaulted by X, and placed in peril of his life, may, if he cannot otherwise repel or avoid the assault, strike X dead. On the one view, the force used by A is both necessary and reasonable; on the other view, the force used by A is employed strictly in self-defence. According to either doctrine A is not justified in shooting at X because X is wilfully trespassing on A's land. For the damage inflicted by A upon X—namely, the risk to X of losing his life—is unreasonable, that is, out of all proportion to the injury done to A by the trespass, and A in firing at a trespasser is clearly using force, not for the purpose of self-defence, but for the purpose of defending his property.

Both theories, again, are consistent with the elaborate and admitted rules which limit a person's right to wound or slay another even in defence of life or limb.

# Understanding Reasonable Force

The gist of these rules is that no man must slay or severely injure another until he has done everything he possibly can to avoid the use of extreme force.

A is struck by a ruffian, X; A has a revolver in his pocket. He must not then and there fire upon X, but, to avoid crime, must first retreat as far as he can. X pursues; A is driven up against a wall. Then, and not till then, A, if he has no other means of repelling attack, may justifiably fire at X. Grant that, as has been suggested, the minute provisos as to the circumstances under which a man assaulted by a ruffian may turn upon his assailant, belong to a past state of society, and are more or less obsolete, the principle on which they rest is, nevertheless, clear and most important. It is, that a person attacked even by a wrongdoer, may not in self-defence use force which is not "necessary", and that violence is not necessary when the person attacked can avoid the need for it by retreat; or, in other words, by the temporary surrender of his legal right to stand in a particular place—e.g. in a particular part of a public square, where he has a lawful right to stand.

Both theories, in short have reference to the use of "necessary" force, and neither countenances the use of any force which is more than is necessary for its purpose.

A is assaulted by X, he can on neither theory justify the slaying or wounding of X if A can provide for his own safety simply by locking a door on X. Both theories equally well explain how it is that as the intensity of an unlawful assault increases, so the amount of force legitimately to be used in self-defence increases also, and how defence of the lawful possession of property, and especially of a man's house, may easily turn into the lawful defence of a man's person.

"A justification of a battery in defence of possession, though it arose in defence of possession, yet in the end it is the defence of the person." This sentence contains the gist of the whole matter, but must be read in the light of the caution insisted upon by Blackstone, that the right of self-protection cannot be used as a justification for attack.

Whether the two doctrines may not under conceivable circumstances lead to different results, is an inquiry of great interest, but in the cases which generally come before the Courts, of no great importance. What usually requires determination is how far a man may lawfully use all the force necessary to repel an assault, and for this purpose it matters little whether the test of legitimate force be its "reasonableness" or its "self-defensive character."

# Understanding Reasonable Force

If, however, it be necessary to choose between the two theories, the safest course for an English lawyer is to assume that the use of force which inflicts or may inflict grievous bodily harm or death—of what, in short, may be called extreme force—is justifiable only for the purpose of strict self-defence. This view of the right of self-defence, it may be objected, restricts too narrowly a citizen's power to protect himself against wrong. The weight of this objection is diminished by two reflections. For the advancement of public justice, in the first place, every man is legally justified in using, and indeed is often bound to use, force, which may under some circumstances amount to the infliction of death.

Hence a loyal citizen may lawfully interfere to put an end to a breach of the peace, which takes place in his presence, and use such force as is reasonably necessary for the purpose.

Hence, too, any private person who is present when any felony is committed is bound by law to arrest the felon, on pain of fine and imprisonment if he negligently permit him to escape.

*"Where a felony is committed and the felon flyeth from justice, or a dangerous wound is given, it is the duty of every man to use his best endeavours for preventing an escape. And if in the pursuit the party flying is killed, where he cannot otherwise be overtaken, this will be*

*deemed justifiable homicide. For the pursuit was not barely warrantable; it is what the law requireth, and will punish the wilful neglect of."*

No doubt the use of such extreme force is justifiable only in the case of felony, or for the hindrance of crimes of violence. But "such homicide as is committed for the prevention of any forcible and atrocious crime, is justifiable . . . by the law of England as it stands at the present day. If any person attempts the robbery or murder of another, or attempts to break open a house in the night-time, and shall be killed in such attempt, either by the party assaulted, or the owner of the house, or the servant attendant upon either, or by any other person, and interposing to prevent mischief, the slayer shall be acquitted and discharged. This reaches not to any crime unaccompanied with force - as, for example, the picking of pockets; nor to the breaking open of a house in the day-time, unless such entry carries with it an attempt of robbery, arson, murder, or the like."

Acts therefore which would not be justifiable in protection of a person's own property, may often be justified as the necessary means, either of stopping the commission of a crime, or of arresting a felon.

Burglars rob A's house, they are escaping over his garden wall, carrying off A's jewels with them. A is in no peril of his life, but he pursues the gang, calls upon them to surrender, and having no other means of preventing their escape, knocks down one of them, who dies of the blow; A, it would seem, if Foster's authority may be trusted, not only is innocent of guilt, but has also discharged a public duty.

Let it be added that where A may lawfully inflict grievous bodily harm upon X—e.g. in arresting him—X acts unlawfully in resisting A, and is responsible for the injury caused to A by X's resistance.

Every man, in the second place, acts lawfully as long as he merely exercises his legal rights, and he may use such moderate force as in effect is employed simply in the exercise of such rights.

A is walking along a public path on his way home, X tries to stop him; A pushes X aside, X has a fall and is hurt. A has done no wrong; he has stood merely on the defensive and repelled an attempt to interfere with his right to go along a public way.

X thereupon draws a sword and attacks A again. It is clear that if A can in no other way protect himself—e.g. by running away from X, or by knocking X down—he may use any amount of force necessary for his self-defence. He may stun X, or fire at X.

Here, however, comes into view the question of real difficulty. How far is A bound to give up the exercise of his rights, in this particular instance the right to walk along a particular path, rather than risk the maiming or the killing of X?

Suppose, for example, that A knows perfectly well that X claims, though without any legal ground, a right to close the particular footpath, and also knows that, if A turns down another road which will also bring him home, though at the cost of a slightly longer walk, he will avoid all danger of an assault by X, or of being driven, in so-called self-defence, to inflict grievous bodily harm upon X.

Of course the case for A's right to use any force necessary for his purpose may be put in this way. A has a right to push X aside. As X's violence grows greater, A has a right to repel it. He may thus turn a scuffle over a right of way into a struggle for the defence of A's life, and so justify the infliction even of death upon X. But this manner of looking at the matter is unsound. Before A is justified in, say, firing at X or stabbing X, he must show distinctly that he comes within one at least of the two principles which justify the use of extreme force against an assailant. But if he can avoid X's violence by going a few yards out of his way, he cannot justify his conduct under either of these principles. The firing at X is not "reasonable," for the damage inflicted by A upon X in wounding him is out of all proportion to the mischief to A which it is intended to prevent—namely, his being forced to go a few yards out of his way on his road home. The firing at X, again, is not done in strict self-defence, for A could have avoided all danger by turning into another path.

A uses force, not for the defence of his life, but for the vindication of his right to walk along a particular pathway.

That this is the true view of A's position is pretty clearly shown by the old rules enjoining a person assaulted to retreat as far as he can before he grievously wounds his assailant.

Reg. v. Hewlett, a case tried as late as 1858, contains judicial doctrine pointing in the same direction. A was struck by X. A thereupon drew a knife and stabbed X. The judge laid down that "unless the prisoner [A] apprehended robbery or some similar offence, or danger to life, or serious bodily danger" (not simply being knocked down) he would not be justified "in using the knife in self-defence."

The essence of this dictum is, that the force used by A was not justifiable, because, though it did ward off danger to A—namely, the peril of being knocked down—it was not necessary for the defence of A's life or limb, or property. The case is a particularly strong one, because it was not a person asserting a supposed right, but a simple wrongdoer.

Let the last case be a little varied. Let X be not a ruffian but a policeman, who, acting under the orders of the Commissioner of Police, tries to prevent A from entering the Park at the Marble Arch. Let it further be supposed that the Commissioner has taken an erroneous view of his authority, and that therefore this attempt to hinder A from going into Hyde Park at the particular entrance does not admit of legal justification. X, under these circumstances, is therefore legally in the wrong, and A may, it would seem, push by X. But is there any reason for saying that if A cannot simply push X aside he can lawfully use the force necessary— e.g. by stabbing X—to effect an entrance? There clearly is none. The stabbing of X is neither a reasonable nor a self-defensive employment of force.

A dispute, in short, as to legal rights must be settled by legal tribunals, "for the King and his Courts are the *vindices injuriarum* and will give to the party wronged all the satisfaction he "deserves"; no one is allowed to vindicate the strength of his disputed rights by the force of his arm. Legal controversies are not to be settled by blows". A bishop who in the last century attempted, by means of riot and assault, to make good his claim to remove a deputy registrar, was admonished from the Bench that his view of the law was erroneous, and was saved from the condemnation of the jury only by the rhetoric and the fallacies of Erskine.

From whatever point therefore the matter be approached, we come round to the same conclusion. The only undoubted justification for the use of extreme force in the assertion of a man's rights is, subject to the exceptions or limitations already mentioned, to be found in, as it is limited by, the necessities of strict self-defence.

The writings of Dicey have been a great source of knowledge for me in my attempt at understanding the legal issues that relate to a person's right to self-defence and the concept of reasonable force.

However, since the inclusion of *The Criminal Law Act 1967* in English Law pre-1967 case law judgements can no longer be relied upon as providing legal authority. Therefore, what we must do now is to look to not only the primary statutes in this area; namely *Section 3(1)* of *The Criminal Law Act 1967* and *Article 2* of *The Human Rights Act 1998,* but also the case-law precedents made by Judges that have developed our common-law rights since the 1967 Act came into force.

Mark Dawes

# Chapter 3
# Current Law in
# Relation to 'Self-Defence'

*"Man perfected by society is the best of all animals;
he is the most terrible of all when he lives without
law, and without justice."*

—Aristotle

## What the Law provides

The 'general rule of law' that relates to the use
of reasonable force can be found in Section 3(1) of
The Criminal Law Act 1967 which states that:

*"Any person may use such force as is reason-
able in the circumstances in preventing a crime, or
in effecting or assisting in the lawful arrest of
offenders or suspected offenders or of persons
unlawfully at large."*

## Statutory Interpretation—Understanding what
the law means

Now one thing we can learn right here is that
the writing of law is its interpretation. This is what

# Understanding Reasonable Force

I call the 'Ronseal' rule. You may recall that Ronseal produces wood preservative products and their sales pitch is that, *"It does exactly what it says on the tin."* In terms of the law the same principle applies. The words used in the Act of Parliament are exactly what it means. In other words what is written is the interpretation.

Another Act of Parliament, *The Interpretation Act 1978*, and related case law, sets statutory rules for determining the meaning and therefore the effect of Acts of Parliament. *The Interpretation Act 1978* requires Acts of Parliament to be construed according to the intention of Parliament, which is to be sought only in the words used in the Act unless they are imprecise or ambiguous. Where the meaning is plain, it is to be adopted. For example the word "may" is permissive and "shall" is imperative.

To illustrate this let's look at the interpretation of the statute law in relation to the use of reasonable force. In *Section 3(1)* of *The Criminal Law Act 1967* it states that "any person *may* use such force..". Therefore, if we interpret the words within the Act, consistent with the rules of statutory interpretation, we can understand exactly what the law requires through the words used in it.

To start with *Section 3(1)* of *The Criminal Law Act* states that *"any person... "*. This means anyone within the country that the law applies in. It then goes on to say *"may use force.."*. The word "may" is a verb that by interpretation gives permission for any person to use force. The Act then goes on to state *"as is reasonable in the circumstances"*—and we will come on to defining what reasonable means in a few moments.

Therefore to summarise so far what *Section 3(1)* of *The Criminal Law Act 1967* means, by its interpretation, is that any individual has the permission (granted by The Act of Parliament) to use force. However, the amount of force is qualified by the word "reasonable" meaning that each and every individual is allowed to use only such force that is "reasonable" in a given set of circumstances.

In short this means that all citizens have the legal permission to use force. However, with that right goes a lawful responsibility to use only such force as is reasonable in a given set of circumstances.

*Section 3(1)* of *The Criminal Law Act 1967* then goes on to state that: *"...in preventing a crime, or in effecting or assisting in the lawful arrest of offenders or suspected offenders or of persons unlawfully at large."* Therefore, provided we are conforming with the use of force to prevent a crime, arresting offenders etc we are acting lawfully within our legal right.

In relation to our right to self-defence or defence of another this Act of Parliament provides, in its interpretation, the right of all citizens to use force in their defence or in the defence of others based on the fact that any infliction of force upon another person may amount to an assault against the person and as such a crime.

Reasonable force however, is not defined any further by the words within the Act of Parliament itself. Further more, whether or not the force used was reasonable or not is dependent on the circumstances of each individual case. Therefore, we can see that defining reasonable is not that easy and its interpretation is somewhat vague. Sadly this is where the knowledge that many people tasked with managing or controlling how others use physical force stops.

However, the clue has already been given. If reasonable is dependent on the circumstances of each individual case, why not look at cases that have been judged in Court under *Section 3(1)* of *The Criminal Law Act 1967?* This way we can find out specifically which judgements have been made in Court as to what is and what is not reasonable. By doing this we can find out what the Courts' definition of reasonable is in differing cases and we can see what 'case law precedents' have been set by the higher Courts which the other Courts have to follow in future judgements. If this is then done for a number of cases a trend will appear and within that trend there will be certain characteristics that will have formed on which future judgements on the use of reasonable force will be based.

By doing this we can develop a working principle of what constitutes reasonableness and what the Courts will look for in future judgements. Once this is done we can then apply these findings to the delivery of training on the subject so that when someone asks what reasonable means we can tell them more specifically the underpinning principles of what constitutes reasonable force and then combine that with real case examples to illustrate the point.

The basis of what follows is based on our research and development. Where appropriate case references are given so that you may do your own due diligence if you so wish and examples have been presented to allow you to see the explanation within given situations. In all cases our examples are based on real events.

**Self Defence & Lawful Excuse[2]**

With regard to *Section 3(1)* of *The Criminal Law Act 1967*, what would otherwise be regarded as criminal conduct is sometimes allowed a lawful excuse and the best known of these is self-defence. Criminal law allows for the protection of basic rights. As a result, an individual who is subject to an attack is accorded the right to repel such an attack by the lawful excuse of self-defence. However, if it is necessary to use force then only a proportionate amount of force is permitted.

As Dicey put it: "The innocent subject of an attack should not be free to use whatever force is

---

[2] Ashworth, Principles of Criminal Law, p137.

necessary to vindicate his threatened rights, this would assign no value to the rights of the attacker. Forfeiture of life to protect a person from some minor hurt, loss or damage would promote honour above respect for life and limb"—this is not what the law is about[3].

## Minimum Force and Least Restrictive Physical Intervention

Now, before getting into the main issue of defining *'reasonable force'* further I thought I would dedicate a few lines to the subject of *'minimum force'* and *'least restrictive physical intervention'* as these are terms that crop up regularly in various organisational guidance documents and corporate/departmental policies in local authorities, residential care homes and various other sources when relating to the use of physical force. This is particularly true when guidance and instruction is given on subjects such as breakaway training and restraint/physical intervention training.

The *'principle'* of minimum force goes beyond, and is more restrictive than what the law requires[4]. *Section 3* of *The Criminal Law Act 1967* requires that "any person may use such force as is reasonable in the circumstances in order to prevent a crime or to arrest an offender."

---

[3] Dicey

[4] "Overkill" or "Minimum Force"? – A paper by P.A.J. Waddington, Ph.D., Director of Criminal Studies, University of Reading.

Therefore, well-meaning managers or employers or trainers or authors of guidance documents, produced in some cases by Government Departments, who actively inform staff that they can only use *'minimum force'* or *'least restrictive physical intervention'* are actually restricting a person's legal right to use reasonable force.

The intention in the use of the words *'minimum force'* is possibly a way of organisations attempting to promote reasonableness and discouraging excessiveness. There are possibly many reasons for this, the need to protect the person whom force is being used on for example, being a primary consideration. It is also true that some organisations believe that staff may 'abuse' their right to use reasonable force so incorporate words such as *'minimum'* and *'least restrictive physical intervention'* as a means of managing the use of force.

The use of such words could also be a way by which some organisations hope to delegate their responsibility with regard to the use of force from the organisation to the member of staff who, as Leadbetter commented on in a report for the Scottish Office which was published in 1997 stated:

> *"The historical tendency has been to individualise... the management of challenging behaviour. To frame it simply as a matter of individual staff competence with risk viewed as simply "part of the job". This perspective has effectively de-emphasised the role and*

> *responsibility of the agency and focused the responsibility for risk assessment and intervention on the individual staff member, who inevitably remains in the frame when things go wrong."*

However, if we look at *The Human Rights Act 1998*, which came into force in October 2000, and which will be covered in more depth in a later chapter, we can see why such delegation may now only serve to increase the liability of the organisation.

In the case of *McCann v United Kingdom [1996] 21 EHRR 97*, the most important ruling was that *Article 2* requires law enforcement operations to be organised so as to *'minimise, to the greatest extent possible, recourse to lethal force'*. In the McCann case the Court found that the planning of the operation failed to show the required level of respect for the subject's right to life. A point to note for any organisational management team here is that the Court ruling did not find the soldiers who fired the fatal shots guilty. It found the State guilty.

Therefore, we shouldn't manage by the use of verbal adjective modifies such as *'minimum'* or *'least restrictive'* alone but by a competent understanding of what the principles of reasonable force are.

In addition, the inference of minimal force will most possibly also leave staff confused and can create a risk in itself if staff actually believe that in defending against a violent assault they are not allowed to cause injury to their attacker, an issue raised on many courses by a high degree of public authority staff. In fact one widely used breakaway video tends to support this doctrine which starts by the presenter stating:

> "Legally if you are the victim of an assault you have every right to try and escape. However, there are potential problems if this entails inflicting injury on the aggressor, so in this programme we are going to explore a range of simple techniques that will enable you to break away should someone lay hands on you. These techniques are designed to be the minimum amount of force required to escape. They are not strikes, kicks or punches. There is no aggressiveness about them. A correctly used breakaway technique will only damage the aggressor's pride."

The above statement seems to infer that legally any person can use force to defend themselves, but they could get in trouble if they hurt their aggressor. Therefore, if we teach you techniques that require a 'minimal amount of force'—not strikes, kicks or punches—then you will be able to defend yourself 'nicely' in a non-aggressive manner should you become the victim of a violent and aggressive assault. As you may be beginning to realise, such instruction is not only stupid but also dangerous, and possibly even illegal.

# Understanding Reasonable Force

In addition, the principle of *'minimum force'* and *'least restrictive physical intervention'* is sometimes promoted in training to encourage staff to use the least harmful technique first and then, if necessary, to escalate up to a more restrictive technique should the initial technique fail, and so on. For interventions that are of low intensity and pose little or no risk, or for defences against a smaller, older and/or less able assailant[5] this may work well. However, for staff expected to defend against or control a physically stronger assailant, especially if the staff member/s are at the low end of the skill spectrum, and/or who may be of mature age having to defend against or attempt to restrain an aggressive assailant who may be younger, stronger and at a higher range in the skill spectrum, the principle of *'minimum force'* and *'least restrictive physical intervention'* will prove unworkable and impracticable that will undoubtedly increase the margin for error and the likelihood of harm to occur.

Therefore, although the 'policy' of *'minimal force'* or *'least restrictive physical intervention'* may be *'socially'* or *'politically'* correct in its intention, it may be lawfully incorrect in its application if taught within a framework that is more restrictive than what the law requires, especially if that imposed restriction breaches the rights provided by law for each individual. If this then leads to

---

[5] The use of the term 'assailant' is purely used to describe anyone attempting to cause physical injury to another and is not intended depiction of a person's criminal intent or character.

staff being injured from trying to implement the restrictive requirements this could lead to action being taken against the organisation for negligence based on unlawful guidance and instruction.

Further more, the proposed implementation of *The Corporate Manslaughter Bill* could leave directors and senior managers open to charges of Gross Negligence Manslaughter should death result from unlawful restrictions being imposed that increased the risk of death.

As opposed to using words in an attempt to control how other individuals may and may not use force why not simply let them understand the true principles of reasonable force by training them properly. In essence all use of force training (self-defence, breakaway and physical intervention/restraint) should have a module on the law included as standard instruction so that staff may understand fully what the law allows and restricts. Mind you, that would probably mean training the trainers and policy makers too and that might cost money!

## Justifiable Lawful Excuses

What must be considered at this point is that every time we touch someone, with the intention of causing harm, technically, we commit a crime by 'assaulting' our 'assailant'. Therefore, some individuals may find themselves in certain circumstances in which they will have to cause harm to prevent harm. An example of this will be if a person is being attacked and they use force to defend themselves which injures their attacker.

The law does recognise however, that in certain situations justification may exist for engaging in conduct which might otherwise give rise to criminal liability and this justification is generally referred to as the defence of lawful excuse.

To bring us more up to date The *Draft Criminal Code*[6] restated six situations when the use of force is justifiable which are listed below:

- To prevent or terminate crime, or to effect or assist in the lawful arrest of an offender or suspected offender or person unlawfully at large.

- To prevent or terminate a breach of peace.

- To protect himself or another from unlawful force or unlawful personal harm - this is self-defence broadened to cover defensive force in support of another person.

- To prevent or terminate the unlawful detention of himself or another.

- To protect property (whether belonging to himself or another) from unlawful appropriation destruction or damage.

---

[6] Law Comm No. 177, clause 44.

- To prevent or terminate a trespass to his person or property.

There is some overlap between these situations, e.g. in most cases where a person is using physical force they may be acting to prevent a crime being committed by an aggressor. However, in some cases only the common law defence will be available, e.g. where the attacker against whom the force used is not committing a crime, for example because they are a child below the age of criminal responsibility.

## Breach of the Peace

As you have seen from the lawful excuses provided any individual may use force to prevent or terminate a breach of peace. To define what constitutes a Breach of the Peace we can again refer to case law on the subject and find the following from the case of *R v. Howell (1982)*:

> *"The Peace is the normal state of society and a Breach of the Peace occurs when harm is done or likely to be done to a person, or in his presence to his property, or a person is in fear of such harm."*

Therefore, if we again use the rules of statutory interpretation in relation to preventing or terminating a breach of the peace we can see that we have lawful excuse to use reasonable force to: a) prevent or terminate harm being done, or likely to be done to a person; b) prevent or terminate harm being caused to a person's property; and, c) prevent or terminate the fear of harm occurring to them from a person threatening to cause such harm.

The point to note above is that force can be used not only to prevent harm that is actually being done but also to prevent the likely harm that may result from a person threatening that such harm could occur. By interpretation therefore, reasonable force can be used pre-emptively and we do not have to wait for the other person to physically assault us first to seek justification to defend ourselves.

Furthermore, in the case of *Albert v Lavin*[7] Lord Diplock stated:

> *"Every citizen in whose presence a breach of the peace is being, or reasonably appears to be about to be, committed has the right to take reasonable steps to make the person who is breaking or threatening to break the peace refrain from doing so; and those reasonable steps in appropriate cases will include detaining him against his will. At common law this is not only the right of every citizen, it is also his duty, although, except in the case of a citizen who is a constable, it is a duty of imperfect obligation."*

---

[7] Albert v Lavin [1982] AC 546.

## What constitutes Reasonable Force?

What the criminal law rules of defence do is try to establish equilibrium between the two extremes of not allowing the victim to use any force at all and, on the other hand, using force without regard to the proportionality of their actions. In relation to the use of force the law today therefore still turns on two basic requirements to determine whether or not force was reasonable. These are:

**Necessity.** In the first instance it must have been necessary to use force. And if so the force used should be:

**Proportionate** to the harm/crime/mischief that the individual is attempting to prevent or terminate. A proportionality standard has developed from the case law, that is, the force used to repel the crime must be proportionate to the force threatened, and we can find examples of judgements made by courts and use these to illustrate proportionate use of force in specific situations which reflect the rights of individuals to exert their lawful excuses.

A point to bear in mind is that if it is not necessary to use force, so force should not be used, then we cannot construct an argument that although we shouldn't have done it the force used was proportionate.

# Understanding Reasonable Force

To further define reasonableness we need to look in more depth at the aspects of necessity and proportionality and these two important factors are further explained below.

## Necessity

In his book, Principles of Criminal Law, Andrew Ashworth[8] attempts to organise the remaining leading cases of self-defence around six aspects of necessity. In doing so Ashworth raises some interesting points not only regarding the aspect of necessity but also with regard to the issue of *'minimal force'* which we discussed earlier.

His six aspects of necessity are identified and further defined as follows:

1. Is the Threat Imminent?
2. There is a duty to avoid conflict—to disengage and to make some physical withdrawal.
3. Protection of the home.
4. Freedom of Movement.
5. The Pre-emptive strike.
6. Necessity & Law Enforcement.

Now we'll look at each one of the above points in further detail.

---

[8] Ashworth, Principles of Criminal Law, p145.

## 1. Is the Threat Imminent?

Defensive force can only be necessary if the attack is imminent or immediate. The reasoning is that if there is time to warn the Police, then that is the course that should be taken, in preference to the use of force by a private individual. But this does not mean that it is unlawful to keep armaments for an anticipated attack in *Attorney General's Reference (No. 2 of 1983)*[9], it was held that it is not illegal to keep weapons in anticipation of a future attack. There is however contradiction between this and the lawfulness of carrying a weapon. In general, I would suggest it best to avoid the carrying of an 'offensive weapon', since under *Evans v Hughes*[10], it was held that while it was necessary to use the weapon during the attack, the carrying of it beforehand remained an offence.

## 2. A Duty to Avoid Conflict

One of the most technical but most significant elements in the common law of self-defence was the duty to retreat. The duty has now disappeared as such. In *Julien (1969)*, it was rephrased as a duty to demonstrate an unwillingness to fight 'to temporise and disengage and perhaps to make some physical withdrawal.'

In *Bird (1985)*, the Court of Appeal accepted that the imposition of a 'duty' is too strong. The

---

[9] [1984] QB 456.
[10] [1972] 3 All ER 412.

key question is whether a person was acting in self-defence or in revenge or retaliation. Evidence that a person was attempting to retreat or withdraw from the area might negate the suggestion of revenge.

If the use of force is unnecessary (e.g. because the initial aggressor has started to retreat) it will not be reasonable in the circumstances to use force.[11]

## 3. Protection of the Home

One longstanding exception to the duty to retreat is that a person attacked at home has no duty to withdraw. In principle, greater force is justifiable if occupation of the home is being threatened unlawfully than if mere personal property is being taken. However, there have been several cases in which a firearm, sword or knife has been used against a burglar which raise questions about the proportionality of the injury done to the value of the interest protected. The cases of Tony Martin and Captain Moir, as previously discussed, are examples of such points and help us understand the legal framework regarding such an issue, yet one can still not help but feel that the Law is biased against law abiding citizens in such cases. However, the a recent case reported in The Times newspaper on Saturday December 7th 2002 does illustrate how the law protects law abiding citizens.

---

[11] Priestnall v Cornish [1979] Crim LR 310, DC.

In this particular case, two burglars, Darren Taylor and Ian Reed, burst through an unlocked door of John and Carol Lambert's bungalow in Spalding Lincolnshire and held a knife at the throat of Mrs Lambert, demanding £5,000.00. While Darren Taylor dragged Mrs Lambert into the bedroom Mr Lambert escaped from Ian Reed by punching him in the face. Mr Lambert then ran into the kitchen and armed himself with a knife before running into the street and shouting for help. Mr Lambert then heard Taylor behind him and a struggle ensued. Mr Lambert told the court: *"He was trying to kill me. I had in my mind that I was going to die. I was quite convinced that Carol and myself were both going to die."*

Taylor and Mr Lambert crashed through a fence and ended up fighting on the ground, when Taylor suffered a fatal knife wound to his chest and slumped back.

After the incident Mr Lambert was arrested on suspicion of murder but all charges were dropped. The jury decided that Mr Lambert had acted in self-defence and returned a verdict of lawful killing.

## 4. Freedom of Movement

English Law also recognises an exception to the 'duty' to avoid conflict in those cases where an individual is acting lawfully in remaining at, or going to, a place, realising that there is a risk that someone will force a violent confrontation there.

# Understanding Reasonable Force

In the case of *Field (1972),* D was warned that some men were coming to attack him. D stayed where he was, the men came and made their attack, and in the ensuing struggle D stabbed one of them fatally. The Court of Appeal quashed his conviction, holding that he had no duty to avoid conflict until his attackers were present and had started to threaten him.

In addition, clearly a person who acts with the purpose of preventing crime or arresting a suspected offender cannot be expected to avoid conflict, and is therefore governed by the proportionality standard.

In the setting of a hospital department for example, this would perhaps include instances where a patient, known to be aggressive, is on a certain ward or in a certain room. Staff are under no duty to avoid the ward, since this would be seen as an infringement of the right to freedom of movement. The idea behind this principle is the avoidance of bullying or terrorising in society, by restricting citizens of where they can go. (However, there are Health and Safety issues involved in providing a safe working environment, safe working practices and systems of work which must be provided for staff if the risk of such an encounter is foreseeable whilst at work).

## 5. Pre-Emptive Strike

The use of force in self-defence may even be justified as a pre-emptive strike, when an unlawful attack is imminent.[12]

This is a desirable rule, and it is consistent with the lawful excuse of preventing or terminating a *Breach of the Peace*, since the rationale for self-defence involves the protection of an innocent citizen's vital interests (life, physical security, etc) and it would be nonsense if the citizen was obliged to wait until the first blow was struck.

Therefore, although a person who acts in self-defence is normally actually being attacked, the defence is not limited to this situation, since it has been recognised that there may be situations in which it will be justified to use reasonable force by way of pre-emptive action against an apprehended attack.[13]

Take for example the situation of a hospital security officer faced with a member of the public brandishing a knife. It is perfectly reasonable for the security officer to strike the member of the public in order to relieve the threat of a knife attack. A criminal law, which failed to provide the security officer this right, would not be adequate.

---

[12] Beckford v R [1988]

[13] A-G's Reference (No.2 of 1983) [1984] 1 All ER 988, CA; Beckford v R [1987] 3 All ER 425, PC).

It should be recognised however that a pre-emptive strike will only be reasonable for example when the defendant has done all he can to avoid the conflict unless of course the conflict could not be avoided. As Dicey put it, a law which allows pre-emptive strikes without any general duty to avoid conflict runs the risk, as of over-stimulating self-assertion.

## 6. Necessity & Law Enforcement

A person whose purpose is to prevent crime or apprehend a suspected offender may also behave pro-actively.

The primary legal restriction on such conduct is the standard of proportionality, in relation to the purpose that the individual was aiming to achieve. For example, how serious an offence was being or had been committed? Is there a real danger of further offending?

If we go back to the issue of minimum force we can see here where the principle starts to break down. If there is to be a social policy of the minimisation of force, it would seem to follow that any person pursuing such a principle should not use force unless necessary, and then only use as little as possible. This may well work in situations where little force is justifiable and where the risk is low or the mischief or crime being committed is minor, such as preventing a young child committing theft who poses no threat of violence, or to arrest someone for minor criminal damage who does not have the ability to put up a violent struggle. In the context of serious violence, however, the policy of minimal force may prove impractical.

For example, some Police are issued with firearms and they are instructed to open fire only in conditions which would justify killing. Should they shoot to kill, or try to wound and disable? The policy of minimal force would suggest the latter, but in practice there are difficulties:

- If the other person is armed, any failure to incapacitate totally may leave the opportunity for a gun to be fired or explosive to be detonated, resulting in the loss of innocent life; and

- It is far more difficult to shoot and hit legs and arms than to shoot at and hit the torso, again making failure and the loss of innocent life more probable.

Therefore, in order to achieve minimal injury and loss of life, it would be best to shoot to kill as soon as the danger to life becomes apparent.

## Proportionality

Having now discussed necessity, the first aspect with regard to reasonableness, we need to now consider the issue of proportionality. This is because even if the force used was justified by its necessity it must still be applied with due regard to the proportionately of the outcome it may produce in relation to the harm it may prevent.

# Understanding Reasonable Force

A proportionality standard has developed from case law. That is, the force used, or the harm caused by the application of such force, must be proportionate to the force threatened or the harm that could have resulted. The standard is best defined in terms of what is reasonably proportionate to the amount of harm likely to be suffered by the defendant or likely to result if the forcible intervention is not made.

To illustrate the above points let me highlight the following two case examples:

## Case Example 1:

A security officer was on duty at a busy hospital when he was called to the A&E department. On arrival he was confronted with a man in a wheelchair who was verbally abusing and inappropriately touching female nursing staff. The security officer was asked to remove the man from the area until he could be seen to prevent further abuse and touching.

On pushing the man out of the A&E department, the man started to verbally abuse and threaten the officer. The officer moved away increasing his distance not believing that any use of force was required at this stage. Due to the man's frustration he leapt out of the wheelchair and began moving towards the officer stating that he was going to *"do him"*. The officer moved further away and with his hands raised in-front of him, palms facing away, gave clear instructions to the man to back away. The man, ignoring the officer's verbal directives carried on heading towards the officer. The officer, now believing the threat to be real, struck the assailant by use of a shin-kick resulting in the assailant going to ground from where he was controlled and attended to by nursing staff.

In this case the police were called and it was considered that the officer's actions were necessary (based on an honestly.held belief) and proportionate to the harm that could have occurred should the attack not have been prevented.

In this case the officer clearly showed an unwillingness to fight, and, when he could retreat no further, resorted to a pre-emptive strike to prevent the attack, which he honestly believed would occur, from occurring. The pre-emptive action was consistent with an unwillingness to fight. It can also be argued that the force used (a shin-kick) was also a proportionate use of force option as the worst harm that could have been inflicted would have been a broken shin, which would have probably and possibly have been less then the harm which may have been suffered by the security officer had the attack not have been prevented.

**Case Example 2:**

Nursing staff on a paediatric ward rush to prevent a fifteen year-old boy from jumping out of one of the ward windows. The ward is located on the fourth floor of the hospital and the window the boy is attempting to jump from is directly above a pavement area and wall. The staff honestly believe that if the boy manages to jump out of the window he is very likely to die. The staff, therefore, quickly grab the boy to prevent him from jumping and in the resulting struggle they all end up on the floor having slipped on some spilt fluid. As a result of the intervention by staff and the subsequent struggle, the boy suffers a broken arm. The question is was the force reasonable in the circumstances, i.e. necessary and proportionate?

Staff responding to such an incident would have believed the use of force was necessary to prevent imminent serous harm and possible death to the boy, so justification can be found on that basis. This then qualifies the necessity question—'But what about proportionality?' The test is that although the action by staff resulted in harm to the boy by way of a broken arm, did their action prevent a greater harm from occurring? In this case, the answer is 'Yes!" and although an injury occurred, it was lesser in proportion than that which could have occurred had staff not intervened and the boy had jumped and therefore, proportionate. Also, the intention of staff was to protect the child and not to cause intentional injury.

# Chapter 4
# The Human
# Rights Act 1998

*"The law hath not been dead, though it hath slept."*

—William Shakespeare (1564 - 1616)

It is at this point that we should stop for a moment and consider the impact and influence of *The Human Rights Act 1998* that came into effect in October 2000 giving every citizen a clear statement of rights and responsibilities.

This is not a new principle, nor is it purely the will of Europe being imposed upon us. To understand the implications of the new Act we need to look back in time, approximately 791 years ago. It was then, on June 15th 1215 that King John, brother to Richard the Lionheart, signed *Magna Carta* at Runnymede to avoid a civil war he would have undoubtedly lost. At that stage in our history every borough, abbey or manor had its charter setting out its own peculiar rights and privileges which even a King was obliged to respect. At Runnymede this concept was, for the first time, extended to the entire country just as our common law was beginning to develop.

*Article 39* of *Magna Carta* states that: *"No freeman shall be taken or imprisoned... save by the lawful judgement of his peers"*, a statement that formed the fundamental principle of a democratic society.

We should also understand that when the Human Rights Act was incorporated in English law it was not merely an Act imposed upon us by Europe claiming new rights to individuals, it was the coming home of a descendant of *Magna Carta* to re-affirm our common law "ancient rights".

## Compatibility by public authorities

*The Human Rights Act* requires that all legislation—Acts of Parliament, Regulations, Orders—so far as is possible, be read and given effect in a way which is compatible with the Convention rights.

All public authorities therefore, have a positive obligation to ensure that respect for human rights is at the core of their day-to-day work. This means that they are expected to act in a way that positively reinforces the principles of *The Human Rights Act*. The Act underpins this by making it unlawful for a public authority to act (or fail to act) in a way which is incompatible with a Convention right. This covers all aspects of the public authority's activities including:

- Drafting rules and regulations

- Internal staff and personnel issues

- Administrative procedures

- Decision making

- Policy implementation

- Interaction with members of the public

*The Human Rights Act* provides individuals with a number of 'protected' rights to enforce their civil liberty and it is now unlawful for any public authority to act in a way which is incompatible with the new rights.

The protection of these rights therefore, in any organisational environment, is the balancing of the economic and business interests of the employer, balanced against the employee's right to be protected from unreasonable demands or restrictions imposed by the employer in pursuit of that business.

# Understanding Reasonable Force

## Article 2—the Right to Life

*Article 2* of *The Human Rights Act* has been described as one of the most fundamental provisions in the Convention as it concerns the protection of all human life. The Article provides for us the positive obligation for public authorities to promote the right to life and it is the primary article that we need to consider when addressing use of physical force.

*Article 2* is a *'Limited Right'* that has two parts to it. Part 1 which promotes the positive obligation that state and public authorities have in promoting the positive obligation to preserve life, and Part 2 which provides the exhaustive (limited) exceptions under which life may be taken if 'absolutely necessary.'

To start with we will look at *Part 1* of *Article 2*.

*Article 2(1) states:*

*"Everyone's right to life shall be protected by law. No one shall be deprived of his life intentionally save in the execution of a sentence of a court following his conviction of a crime for which this penalty is provided by law."*

What this means is that no-one can have their life taken away from them as their life is protected by law and all state authorities and public authorities must take positive steps to promote the positive obligation to preserve life of all people.

This means is that if a terrorist detonates a bomb, with the intention of killing innocent people, does so and is subsequently caught, charged and found guilty of murder in a Court of Law, the Judge cannot pass the death sentence as the Court, as a state/public authority, must promote the positive obligation to preserve life of the criminal.

Therefore, if a Judge (as a Public Official) cannot take the life of a convicted murderer, due to the Court's (as a Public Office) legal requirement to comply with *Article 2* of *The Human Rights Act,* then no other person (or public authority/organisation) may intentionally or recklessly take the life of anyone else. Indeed, due to the requirements of *Article 2(1),* all state/public authorities must take positive steps to ensure that the right to life is upheld where a known risk to life is foreseeable.

*Article 2* suggests that since the right to life is a basic right it should only be taken away when 'absolutely necessary'.

As a result *Part 2 of Article 2 [Article 2(2)]* states that:

*"Deprivation of life shall not be regarded as inflicted in contravention of this Article when it results from the use of force which is no more than absolutely necessary:*

- *In defence of any person from unlawful violence.*

# Understanding Reasonable Force

- *In order to affect a lawful arrest or prevent the escape of a person lawfully detained.*

- *In action lawfully taken for the prevention of quelling a riot or insurrection".*

What this means is the positive obligation to preserve life required by *Article 2(1)* is limited and that life can only be taken, which will not be in contravention of the Article, if it results from the use of force which is no more than *'absolutely necessary'* for the three limited and exhaustive exceptions provided above.

This article states quite clearly that everybody's right to life is protected, and that as such everybody has the lawful right to protect themselves from acts of unlawful violence against them [Part 2 sub-section a). This has a direct bearing on the use of reasonable force. However, we should bear in mind that this exception is generally confined to the use of force for the preservation of life where no other lesser option to preserve life exists.

The standard that has applied up until the Human Rights Act came into force in England and Wales allowed for the use of force where such force is *'reasonable in the circumstances'* (Section 3(1) of The Criminal Law Act 1967). The reasonableness of the use of force has to be decided on the basis of the facts which the user of the force honestly believed to exist—a subjective test, and the responsibility for this subjectivity test rests with the individual.

The test in *Article 2* of the HRA is different and imposes a higher standard. The standard in the Convention is whether the use of force was *'absolutely necessary'*. This is an objective test and places the responsibility firmly at the foot of the state or public authority[14].

As we have seen already we can deprive someone of their life in certain circumstances which would not be in breach of *Article 2*, provided that the force used was no more than *'absolutely necessary'* and this is not defined further by the Act itself. Therefore, just as we did with *'reasonable force'*, we need to seek further clarification of what *'absolutely necessary'* means by reference to case law to find how Courts have interpreted its meaning.

## Stewart v United Kingdom

In *Stewart v United Kingdom*[15] a 13 year-old boy was accidentally killed by a plastic bullet fired into a crowd by the army when trying to quell a riot. The Commission held that this was not a violation of *Article 2* as the force fell within the

---

[14] Although the Act itself gives no definitions of what would constitute a public authority a broad interpretation would include all agencies directly governed by Government, central and local such as the Courts and Police. It could also include 'quasi-public' authorities such as private companies who undertake public duties or who work with the public directly such as some private security companies, private care homes and NHS Trusts.

[15] Stewart v United Kingdom (1984) 38 DR 162.

category of *"absolutely necessary"*. It stated that the force is absolutely necessary if it is strictly proportionate to the achievement of the permitted purpose.

The Commission explained further by stating: *"In assessing whether the use of force is strictly proportionate, regard must be had to the nature of the aim pursued, the dangers to life and limb inherent in the situation and the degree of risk that the force may result in the loss of life."*

The Commission found that the exceptions included in *Article 2(2)* indicate that this provision extends to, but is not concerned exclusively with, intentional killing. It stated that *Article 2*, when read as a whole, indicates that *paragraph 2: "does not primarily define situations where it is permitted intentionally to kill an individual, but defines the situations where it is permitted to 'use force' which may result, as an unintended outcome of the use of force, in the deprivation of life."*

The latter part of the last paragraph provides us with an interesting interpretation. Where it states that it *'defines the situations where it is permitted to use force which may result, as an unintended outcome of the use of force, in the deprivation of life'*. The interpretation of this means that provided an individual was following a proportionate use of force intervention or defence, and death occurs as an unintended outcome, a defence exists in so much as the death was unintended. An example could be an individual who goes to the defence of a person who is being strangled against a wall by a stronger assailant. What the individual does in stopping the attack is grab the assailant by his shoulders and pull him backwards in an attempt to release his grip on the person being strangled. In this case I think we could agree that the force used was proportionate. However, as he pulls the assailant backwards the assailant slips and falls against the side of a desk whereby he bangs his head quite severely and subsequently dies as a result of the injury sustained.

In this example, although the assailant died it could be argued that the intention was not to kill, it was to stop the assailant from harming the other person further by stopping the attack. This could possibly be supported by the application of force which was that the assailant was pulled away from the person being attacked, therefore, the force used was proportionate to the harm being prevented (i.e. strangling could have resulted in the death of the victim and minimum inconvenience or harm was caused to the assailant by pulling him away from his victim). However, the fact that the assailant slipped and fell backwards hitting his head on the desk and subsequently dying was, in this example, *'an unintended outcome of the use of force'* which resulted in the deprivation of life. Therefore, in this case if the defendant was charged with the death of the assailant the defendant would most certainly be able to raise the defence provided in *Stewart v United Kingdom* whereby it could be argued that the defendant was following a proportionate use of force intervention and death resulted as an unintended outcome.

Now, this is not a loop-hole whereby public authorities or companies can decide not to train staff competently and rely on the above case to provide them with a useable defence should death result from lack of organisational control and training, and this is illustrated in the next case.

To understand further the implications of the duty to provide the positive obligation to preserve life we need to refer to the controversial case of *McCann v United Kingdom*[16] which was referred to earlier, involving the shooting and killing of three members of the Provisional IRA by soldiers of the Army's Special Air Service Regiment.

## McCann v United Kingdom

The key issue in this case is that the court not only looked at the decisions made and actions taken by the SAS soldiers who pulled the trigger which led to the deaths of the three members of the Provisional IRA, but also the planning and control of the actions by the state.

In the judge's summing up of the case he stated: *"In making any decision a Court will take into consideration not only the actions of staff who actually administer the force but also the surrounding circumstances including such matters as the planning and control of the actions under examination. This idea of planning and control is important. The Court held that 'the state (in the case of McCann v*

---

[16] McCann v United Kingdom [1995] 21 EHRR 97

*United Kingdom [1995] 21 EHRR 97) must give appropriate training, instructions and briefing to its agents who are faced with a situation where the use of lethal force is possible. The state must also exercise 'strict control' over any operations that may involve the use of lethal force."*

How does this case law affect public authorities? Well for 'state' substitute 'public authority' and for 'agents' substitute 'staff'.

In the McCann case the court not only looked at the decision making and actions by those who pulled the trigger which led to the deaths, but at the planning process, the training and the protection offered by the state.

The violation of *Article 2* came not from those who pulled the trigger but from the fact that the preparation and training was inadequate. One of the key issues was whether these individuals should have been let into Gibraltar in the first place, or whether they should have been arrested earlier?

Points to consider therefore, under new powers given to them in statute must be:

*'That if 'state/public authorities' know what the problem is and fail to adequately deal with it, then that is a failure under Article 2 if that failure leads to a subsequent death, and; if that death could have been prevented, there is bound to be a violation of Article 2.'*

# Understanding Reasonable Force

With regard to the use of physical force as an inclusion in staff safety training programmes this has direct bearings on all organisations that provide this type of training for staff who may be exposed to the risk of a violent assault or who are expected to physically control others. When considering any form of physical skills training the question has to now be addressed as to whether there are ways by which the need for staff and others to be exposed to such risks, and as such the requirement to use physical force, can be eliminated or reduced to its lowest possible factor/risk level by alternative means.

An example of this came out of a meeting that I was recently asked to attend at a local authority to discuss the need to provide a physical skills training programme for staff who work in the community and who undertake home visits.

When I asked specifically what the training was required to do and why it was needed I was informed by the manager that staff had been physically assaulted, threatened with knives and other forms of weaponry, and in one instance a member of staff had been threatened with a gun. As a result the management had decided that they wanted a course that would allow their staff to 'breakaway' if physically attacked. When I asked what they understood by the term 'breakaway' I was informed that they only wanted their staff to be able to use the minimal amount of force necessary to allow them to breakaway from someone who is physically assaulting them. However, they didn't want staff to be taught any skills or techniques that might actually cause any injury or harm to their attacker as if they did it would breach the organisation's policy and the member of staff could be disciplined as a result.

Implementing the principles required by *The Human Rights Act,* and in particular *Article 2(1),* the need to promote the positive obligation to preserve life, I explained to the manager, as politely as I could, that as they knew which individuals posed the risk that it would possibly be much better if staff didn't visit those premises therefore eliminating the risk at source.

*'Can't do that',* said the manager. *'They have to go, we've no choice'.*

*'Ok',* I said, *'but maybe we should look at what type of appropriate lawful force options staff should be given within the training if they are being exposed to potentially life threatening situations'.*

I then proceeded to brief him on what the law required consistent with *Article 2(2)* of T*he Human Rights Act* and what *Section 3(1)* of *The Criminal Law Act 1967* provided. Within the space of an hour it was decided that teaching staff to defend themselves whilst continuing to intentionally expose them to a very serious risk was not only going to possibly breach their Human Rights but also increase the liability of the organisation, and possibly the manager. Furthermore, if they were to pursue training based on their policy of staff using minimum force then the organisation was restricting the legal rights that staff have beyond what is provided for them in statute and common law, and if training were to be delivered on the basis of providing strategic force options that are not consistent with a person's rights, and that inconsistency leads to a death that could have been prevented, especially where the organisation is aware of the risk, then the organisation, and its management, may be taken to Court and charged with a Violation of *Article 2.*

Now for those of you that have got this far well done. As you may be starting to see this is not rocket science.

Next we'll explore the defences available to each and every one of you.

# Chapter 5
# Defences to
# Charges of Assault

*"I disapprove of what you say, but I will defend to the death your right to say it."*

—Voltaire (1694 - 1778)

This chapter is written to look at some of the general defences that are available to us in relation to the use of reasonable force and written to support what you have read in the previous chapters.

There are however, a vast number of different defences that can be raised by lawyers should a case go to Court which are dependent upon the charge brought. These would be too many to list here as to do that we would have to list all of the offences that an individual could be charged with and fall outside the scope of this book. However, if you are interested in knowing more about this specific area then there are a number of excellent reading resources which can be found in the reference section to this book.

# Understanding Reasonable Force

## Justifiable Force and The Emotions

It is well known that a sudden threat to one's own physical safety may lead to strong emotions of fear and panic, producing physiological changes, which take the individual out of his or her 'normal self'.

Therefore, what the law has to ascertain is whether the use of force was an innocent and instinctive reaction, or was it the product of revenge and/or retaliation?

As we have already seen, the case law of Palmer provides us with a working example of an actual case where this aspect was raised.

## Honestly Held Belief

The general approach of the law is that it allows such force to be used as is reasonable in the circumstances, as the defendant believes them to be, even if his belief was a mistaken one and (if so) even if his mistake was an unreasonable one.

The reasonableness of the defendant's belief is relevant, then, only to the question whether the belief was in fact held. (Based on the facts as you subjectively believed them to be).

For example, I pride myself on having a sense of humour. So let's imagine that after a day's work I hide behind your car and as you go to get in it I sneak up behind you, grab you and make you jump. Thinking that you are being attacked you swing your elbow behind you in an attempt to defend yourself and in doing so you make contact with my face and break my nose. Afterwards, when you realise that it was only me messing around you may realise that you made a mistake. However, it was possibly an honest mistake based on what you honestly thought was happening at that moment in time. Therefore, even if afterwards you realised that your belief was mistaken and that the force you used was unreasonable you still have a defence based on the defence of an honestly held belief.

## The 'Uplifted Knife'

The fairness of this concession to what Blackstone termed 'the passions of the human mind' is often supported by reference to the famous dictum of Holmes J., namely that *'detached reflection cannot be demanded in the presence of an uplifted knife'.*

This dictum is significant for its limited application, i.e., typically sudden and grave threats or attacks; it has no application to cases where the attack is known to be imminent and the defendant has time to consider his position. Nor should it necessarily be conclusive in relation to those who are trained to deal with extreme situations, such as the police and the army.

# Understanding Reasonable Force

## Crown Prosecution Service Charging Standards

We all hear horror stories of people defending themselves and/or their property and then being charged with a crime themselves. What we don't hear about are the vast number of cases that do not make the newspaper headlines. Remember, to sell newspapers editors need sensational headlines to promote their own ideology through their press, therefore, a story about someone being charged with assault when protecting themselves or their property will sell newspapers. What you don't see is the fact that many of these cases never reach Court or the cases where people have defended themselves and/or their property and no charges have been brought. In fact many receive commendations for doing so by local Councillors, Mayors and the Police.

As you may already know the Police investigate allegations of crime, gather evidence and where the evidence supports the facts in a criminal investigation, they will make an arrest. However, it is up to the Crown Prosecution Service (CPS) to decide whether or not any charges should be brought as they are the lawyers—not the Police.

To assist you in understanding what the CPS look for I have met with the CPS and as a result of that meeting I have obtained their charging standards[17]. The following is an extract from them. It

---

[17] CPS Offences Against the Person Charging Standard 26 April 1996 – Agreed by the Police and The Crown Prosecution Service'.

helps to shed some light on the current myths that abound with regard to the use of physical force in self-defence and the protected rights of the individual in defending themselves from an unlawful assault.

**CPS Offences Against the Person Charging Standard 26 April 1996—Agreed by the Police and The Crown Prosecution Service.**

*Chapter 12 – Defences to Assaults*

Police officers and prosecutors must consider all assaults in the context in which they are allegedly committed. There will be cases in which the surrounding circumstances will be of help in deciding to bring criminal proceedings.

Particular care must be taken in dealing with cases of assault where the allegation is made by a "victim" who was, at the time, engaged in criminal activity himself. For instance, a burglar who claims to have been assaulted by the occupier of the premises concerned.

It is lawful for an individual to use reasonable force in the following circumstances:

- In self-defence; or
- To defend another; or
- To defend property; or
- To prevent crime; or
- To lawfully arrest.

# Understanding Reasonable Force

Where the use of force in any of these circumstances is reasonable, the "assailant" has an absolute defence and charges relating to the assault should not be brought.

In assessing the reasonableness of the force used, two questions should be asked:

- Was the force justified in the circumstances? (i.e., was there a need for any force at all?) and;

- Was the force used excessive in the circumstances?

The courts have indicated that both questions are to be answered on the basis of the facts as the accused **honestly believed** them to be. To that extent it is a **subjective** test.

12.6 There can be a fine line, however, between what constitutes reasonable and unreasonable force. When considering whether the force used was reasonable or excessive, it is important to consider the words of Lord Morris in Palmer v R [1971] A.C. 814 (a full summary of the case can be found towards the end of this chapter) which emphasise the difficulties often facing someone confronted by an intruder or defending himself against attack:

"If there has been an attack so that defence is reasonably necessary, it will be recognised that a person defending himself cannot weigh to a nicety the exact measure of his defensive action. If the jury thought that in a moment of unexpected anguish a person attacked had only done what he honestly and instinctively thought necessary that would be most potent evidence that only reasonable defensive action had been taken..."

12.7 Where the police are in doubt about whether a charge should be brought in cases such as these, they should seek the advice of the CPS before charging the defendant.

Therefore, as we can see from the CPS's own charging standards:

- Particular care should be taken in dealing with cases of assault where the allegation is made by someone who was at the time committing a criminal offence themselves.

- You can use force in self-defence, to defend another, to defend property or to prevent crime and/or to lawfully arrest (these are your lawful excuses).

- Where the use of force in any of these circumstances is reasonable, you, as the "assailant" (remember if we use force against another person we are 'technically' committing an assault unless we have a lawful excuse) have an absolute defence and charges relating to the assault should not be brought.

- Both questions in relation to the amount of force used in the circumstances are to be answered on the basis of the facts as the accused honestly believed them to be.

- You are not required to weigh up the niceties of law when faced with an attack against your person.

- And if the Police are not sure about whether a charge should be brought they should seek the advice of the CPS before charging you.

## USE OF FORCE IN SELF-DEFENCE—CASE LAW —PALMER v R [1971] AC 814 (PC)

LORD MORRIS OF BORTH-Y-GEST: In their Lordships' view the defence of self-defence is one which can be and will be readily understood by any jury. It is a straightforward conception. It involves no abstruse legal thought. It requires no set words by way of explanation. No formula need be employed in reference to it. Only common sense is needed for its understanding. It is both good law and good sense that a man who is attacked may defend himself. It is both good law and good sense that he may do, but may only do, what is reasonably necessary. But everything will depend upon the particular facts and circumstances. Of these a jury can decide. It may in some cases be only sensible and clearly possible to take some simple avoiding action. Some attacks may be serious and dangerous. Others may not be. If there is some relatively minor attack it would not be common sense to permit some action of retaliation which was wholly out of proportion to the necessities of the situation. If an attack is serious so that it puts someone in immediate peril then immediate defensive action may be necessary. If the moment is one of crisis for someone in imminent danger he may have to avert the danger by some instant reaction. If the attack is all over and no sort of peril remains then the employment of force may be by way of revenge or punishment or by way of paying off an old score or may be pure aggression. There may be no longer any link with a necessity of defence. Of all these matters the good sense of a jury will be the arbiter. There are no prescribed words which must be employed in or adopted in a summing up. All that is needed is a clear exposition, in relation to the particular facts of the case, of the conception of necessary self-defence. If there has been no attack then clearly there will have been no need for defence. If there has been attack so that defence is reasonably necessary it will be recognised that a person defending himself cannot weigh to a nicety the exact measure of his necessary defensive action. If a jury thought that in a moment of unexpected anguish a person attacked had only done what he honestly and instinctively thought was necessary that would be most potent evidence that only reasonable defensive action had been taken. A jury will be told that the defence of self-defence, where the evidence makes its raising possible, will only fail if the prosecution show beyond doubt that what the accused did was not by way of self-defence. But their Lordships consider that if the prosecution have shown that what was done was not done in self-defence then that issue is eliminated from the case. If the jury consider that an accused acted in self-defence or if the jury are in doubt as to this then they will acquit. The defence of self-defence either succeeds so as to result in an acquittal or it is disproved in which case as a defence it is rejected.

The above case law demonstrates and illustrates our rights and responsibilities as contained in common law by a judicial precedent. As we have already seen the CPS refer to this case in its charging standards and courts will be bound to look at the principles of this case when considering future cases where the defence of self-defence is raised.

# Chapter 6
# Health & Safety
# & Duty of Care

*"The best car safety device is a rear-view mirror with a cop in it."*
—Dudley Moore (1935-2002)

As we have already seen the right exists in law for individuals to use reasonable force in their defence or in the defence of others. However, one of the main principles of this right is the responsibility of individuals to exercise that right with due consideration for the balancing of harms. In other words, as Dicey once put it, restricting the urge to place over-stimulated self-assertion where a more appropriate solution can be found.

With regard to employed staff this places a liability on the employer to find ways of eliminating or reducing the need to use physical force by the elimination or reduction of hazards that may give rise to the need for employed staff to use force for their defence.

# Understanding Reasonable Force

For issues that involve a risk to life this is a fundamental requirement for compliance with the positive obligation to preserve life as provided by *The Human Rights Act 1998.*

For example, if employed staff are to be taught a system of physical defence (breakaway etc.) that involves the use of reasonable force then it must be appreciated that the skills being taught are not a pre-requisite to allow employers to expose staff to the risk of violence by merely providing a form of 'self-defence' training.

The basis of British health and safety law is *The Health and Safety at Work etc Act 1974* which sets out the general duties which employers have towards employees and members of the public, and employees have to themselves and to each other.

Some duties are qualified in the Act by the principle of *'so far as is reasonably practicable'.* In other words, the degree of risk in a particular job or workplace needs to be balanced against the time, trouble, cost and physical difficulty of taking measures to avoid or reduce the risk. What the law requires here is what good management and common sense would lead employers to do anyway: that is, to look at what the risks are and take sensible measures to tackle them.

Examples of Sections of the Act that are qualified by the term *'reasonably practicable'* are as follows:

*Section 2 of The Health and Safety at Work Act 1974 states:*

> *"It shall be the duty of every employer to ensure so far as is reasonably practicable the health and safety and welfare of all their employees."*

*Section 3 of The Health and Safety at Work Act 1974 states:*

> *"It shall be the duty of every employer to conduct his undertaking in such a way as to ensure so far as is reasonably practicable that persons not in his employment are not exposed to risks to their health and safety."*

Other Sections of the Act are qualified by the word *'necessary'*. The word necessary imposes a stricter obligation on the employer than reasonably practicable. The word 'necessary' is qualified as doing everything physically possible regardless of cost. An example of one such Section qualified by the word *'necessary'* is as follows:

*Section 2(2)(c) of The Health and Safety at Work Act etc 1974:*

> *"...imposes a duty on every employer to ensure that staff receive information, instruction, training and supervision as is necessary to ensure the Health, Safety and Welfare of staff whilst at work".*

What this means is that if it is *'reasonably practicable'* to train someone as a risk control measure as part of the employers duty of care towards them or others, the argument for risk v cost has been decided in favour of training which becomes a *necessary* requirement. If the employer however, decides not to train due to lack of money there is the potential for failing to ensure that the duty of care is fulfilled.

*The Management of Health and Safety at Work Regulations 1999* (the Management Regulations) generally make it more explicit what employers are required to do to manage health and safety under *The Health and Safety at Work Act*. Like the Act, they apply to every work activity. Where the Act lays out what is required in general terms the Management Regulations provide more specific information as to how it should be done. Therefore, to satisfy the requirement for the organisation to provide a duty of care to staff and others as provided by the Health and Safety at Work Act the organisational management must comply with the requirements of the Management Regulations more specifically.

The main requirement of *The Management of Health and Safety at Work Regulations 1999* is for the employer to carry out a risk assessment on any activity that is hazardous. Employers with five or more employees are not only required to carry out such assessments (undertaken by suitably qualified persons), but are also required to record the significant findings of the risk assessment.

If there is a foreseeable risk of employed staff being exposed to the risk of physical assault, or if staff are expected to use reasonable force to physically control another person, then the risk assessment must show that all reasonable and practicable steps have been taken, to eliminate and/or reduce staff being exposed to the hazard.

There are five basic steps to risk assessment which are:

1) Identify Hazards
2) Identify those people who may be harmed
3) Evaluate the risk
4) Document the Findings
5) Review the assessments

**Hierarchy of Control**

When considering implementing risk management/risk control measures as part of Step 3 (Evaluating the risk) there is a hierarchy of control that can be applied which is identified below as ERICPD.

**E** =Eliminate
**R** =Reduce (Requires an assessment of risk)
**I** =Isolate
**C** =Control
**P** =Personal Protective Equipment (PPE)
**D** =Discipline

# Understanding Reasonable Force

**Eliminate** = In the first instance can the risk or hazard be eliminated at source. In other words if we can remove staff from the hazard or the hazard from staff we eliminate the exposure to the risk. An example would be preventing staff from going to a location knowing that violence is likely to occur there. This is also consistent with the legal principle of 'Necessity' and the 'Unwilling-ness to fight'.

**Reduce** = If the risk cannot be eliminated then a suitable and sufficient assessment of risk must be carried out by a competent person to reduce the risk to its lowest practicable level. This does not require that the risk be eliminated only reduced so far as is reasonably practicable. This would include provision of training, adequate staffing arrangements, etc.

**Isolate** = As part of the risk reduction requirements we may have to consider whether the hazard can be isolated or whether we can isolate staff from the risk if the risk becomes apparent. For example this may mean ensuring that staff can leave and go to a place of safety or, if necessary, whether the hazard can be isolated by temporarily locking them in a room for example whilst awaiting the arrival of trained staff able to control the aggressive person.

**Control** = If staff are required to control an aggressive/violent individual then they need to be competently trained to do so as to minimise the risk to staff and also the person being restrained (Sections 2 and 3 of the Health and Safety at Work Act 1974).

**Personal Protective Equipment** = Staff may also be issued with personal protective equipment or provision and use of work equipment an example of which could be personal attack alarms. However, these should be the last resort in controlling risk and issued when all other hierarchical options have been implemented.

**Discipline** = Finally, if staff fail to operate with the safe systems of work provided for them, or if they decide to ignore the systems and procedures provided for them which creates risk to themselves and / or others then they should be disciplined in line with the organisation's policies and procedures.

With regard to the use of reasonable force once all preventative measures have been exhausted, or it is simply not practical to prevent interaction that could expose staff to the risk of violence, then, and only then, should an appropriate and effective form of physical skill be taught.

## Changes in the Regulations

Mounting pressure from the European Commission forced the Government to agree to amend the legislation that historically banned UK workers from taking civil action against employers. The old legislation prohibited employees from taking civil legal proceedings against employers who fail to comply with their duties under *The Management of Health & Safety at Work Regulations 1999*.

A consultation document; published by the Health and Safety Commission in November 2001 (CD177), set out proposals to amend the so-called 'civil liability exclusion' in MHSWR to allow employees to claim damages from their employer where they have suffered injury or illness as a result of the breach of the Regulations by the employer. For example where an employee fails to undertake a suitable and sufficient risk assessment.

However, on the 27th October 2003 the Office of the Deputy Prime Minister, the Department for Work and Pensions and the Health and Safety Executive announced new regulations to amend *The Health and Safety at Work Regulations 1999 (SI 1999 3242)*.

The new regulations that came into force on 27 October 2003 allow employees to claim damages from their employer in a civil action if they have suffered injury or illness as a result of their employer breaching the 1999 Regulations.

Employers will also be allowed to bring action against their employees for breach of their duties under the 1999 Regulations.

In addition to the requirement to undertake risk assessments, compliance of the *Management of Health and Safety at Work Regulations (MHSW) 1999* requires employers to make arrangements *"for the effective planning, organisation, control, monitoring and review of the preventative and protective measures"* which are to be undertaken. These obligations also extend to temporary workers.

**Procedures for Serious & Imminent Danger**

One Regulation contained in the Management Regulations that provides a hierarchy of options is *Regulation 8.2 (Procedures for Serious or Imminent Danger and for Danger Areas)*, which states:

(a) So far as is practicable, require any persons at work who are exposed to serious and imminent danger to be informed of the nature of the hazard and of the steps taken or to be taken to protect from it.

(b) Enable the persons concerned (if necessary by taking appropriate steps in the absence of guidance or instruction and in the light of their knowledge and the technical means at their disposal) to stop work and immediately proceed to a place of safety in the event of their being exposed to serious, imminent and unavoidable danger; and,

(c) Save in exceptional cases for reasons duly sustained (which cases and reasons shall be specified in those procedures), require the persons concerned to be prevented from resuming work in any situation where there is still a serious and imminent danger.

This particular regulation seems to mirror the responsibility bestowed upon us by the Criminal and Common Law in relation to the use of physical force for defensive purposes. This is an important factor for employers to understand as it promotes the right of staff to be made aware of the nature of the hazards they may be exposed to and what steps they need to take to protect them from it, including the right to remove themselves from a situation of imminent danger and not being required to return whilst that danger is continually present. If they are expected to remain or return then reasons must be specified in written procedures which would require a suitable and sufficient risk assessment to be undertaken.

Certainly, any training that staff may have received to avoid injury as result of an aggressive or violent interaction would certainly reduce the employer's risk of liability in respect of personal injuries received in this way. However, every employer when entrusting tasks to his employees must take into account their capabilities as regards health and safety as required by *Regulation 13* of *The Management of Health & Safety at Work Regulations 1999*. This means that staff must be capable of being able to use the skills they have been taught. This means that the training provided must take into account the ability, age, sex of the person being trained balanced against the ease or difficulty of the skills they are required to learn, their motivation (or lack of) to learn the skills, the amount of skills being taught and the period of time they are allowed to learn them in. (This will be covered in other publications).

However, an employer cannot remove their vicarious liability totally by the provision of training. The recent House of Lords decision in Lister v Hesley Hall highlights this fact and also represents a major change in the law of vicarious liability.

Previously, the well-established law stated that the more heinous the employee's act, the less likely it could be considered to be something for which the employer could be liable, on the grounds that it was less likely to be "in the course of employment". The Lister case seems to be a reversal of that view, and may have a great many ramifications, some of which are yet to be revealed.

The case involves a claim for personal injury against the company, Hesley Hall Ltd, with regard to a charge of negligence based on the acts of one of the company's employees, on the basis that the company was vicariously liable for his negligent action that led to the injuries sustained.

This much can be gathered from the facts of the case, which consisted of a series of personal injury claims brought by former pupils of a school where they had been systematically abused by the housemaster (G). The claim was made against the school, on the grounds that the school was vicariously liable for the actions of G and, therefore, liable for the personal injury inflicted upon them. It was recognised by the House of Lords that G's actions were an abuse of the special position in which the school had placed him (to enable it to discharge its responsibilities).

Only by placing him in that position was G able to carry out the abuse, and he could not have done so had the school not placed him in a position of trust. The school was therefore, vicariously liable for those acts.

The Lords decision in the above case stressed that attention must be given to the close connection between the acts of the employer and the duties he is engaged to perform. The decision took into account the fact that the torts had been committed in the time and on the premises of the defendant while the warden had also been busy caring for the children

This decision has now created a new benchmark in an Employer's liability with regard to the acts of its employees drawing on the close connection between an employed person's position and the acts in which he is engaged to perform.

Whilst this decision is likely to have an immediate and substantial impact on those organisations that care for the young and the vulnerable— a wide ranging group including; schools, nursing homes, prisons, colleges, sheltered accommodation etc.—the overall effects are likely to be wide ranging.

A consideration of the reasoning behind the judgement suggests that an employer may be liable for any wrongful acts committed by an employee (for example breaches of *The Human Rights Act, Health and Safety Statute, etc.,*) if it was the fact of his or her employment which provided the opportunity for the act to be committed.

Therefore, employers should consider carefully whether their organisation could place employees in this kind of position, identify any risks, and identify the best means of guarding against those risks. In short, carrying out a suitable and sufficient risk assessment.

# Chapter 7
# The Financial Cost
# of Negligent Liability

*"It is ignorance of the law rather than knowledge of it that leads to litigation."*

—Cicero (106-43BC) *De legibus 1.6*

Failure to assess foreseeable risks to staff leave the company open to liability arising out of claims made by injured parties. Today the vast majority of local authorities, social care departments, NHS trusts, security agencies and other public authorities and private companies are taking unnecessary risks that will increase their liability.

The biggest risk that many take is in using training providers or sub-contractors who do not have adequate insurance cover for the activity that they are proposing to teach. This creates a massive liability as you will see from the first case below. All organisations have a responsibility to provide a positive duty of care to their staff, and part of that duty of care is in ensuring that training providers and sub-contractors have the correct insurance in place.

In the introduction to *The Management of Health and Safety at Work Regulations 1999 (Approved Code of Practice and Guidance)* it states:

> "If people are working under the control and direction of others are treated as self-employed for tax and national insurance purposes they may nevertheless be treated as their employees for health and safety purposes. It may therefore be necessary to take appropriate action to protect them ... a legal duty under section 3 of the Health and Safety at Work etc Act 1974 (HSW Act) cannot be passed on by means of a contract and there will still be duties towards others under section 3 of the HSW Act."

### £2.1 Million for injury to a wrestler against his (national level) coach's insurance

In May 2002 a landmark decision in an Australian court led to an award of AUD$5.7million (£2.1m) for injury to a wrestler against his (national level) coach's insurance. The court ruled that the wrestler's irreversible spinal injury caused during a training bout was a result of improper supervision. This is expected to set an international precedent for future actions in the courts and it would be naïve to think that it-couldn't happen in the United Kingdom. *(Reported in the UK Sports Coach Membership Newsletter— July 2002.)*

As a result of this case many insurers withdrew from the sport coach market and today it is very difficult to get insurance for occupational physical skill instruction. If you are a commissioner of training I would sincerely advise you to only use training providers who have Employer and Public Liability insurance with specific inclusion for occupational physical skill training.

## Teacher attacked by pupil awarded £190,000

A teacher who was attacked by a dangerous teenage pupil at a special school won £190,000 damages in the High Court. The judge ruled that the London Borough of Newham was negligent for not revealing the need for fuller restraint of the pupil. *(Reported in The Daily Mail, 27 March 2002.)*

## £324,000 payout to family of man who died in custody.

The family of a man who died after being arrested by police won a £324,000 payout from Scotland Yard. Richard O'Brien, 37, died in April 1994 after being pinned to the ground by three officers who said they were arresting him for being drunk and disorderly. Mr O'Brien suffered injuries in 31 areas including 12 cuts to the face and head. In 1995, an inquest jury found the 19 stone father of seven had been "unlawfully killed"; three officers stood trial for his manslaughter in 1999 and were acquitted. *(Reported in The Daily Mail, Tuesday, 14 May 2002.)*

At the inquest the coroner, Sir Montague Levine, said the case reflected "an appalling lack of instruction" among officers in restraint techniques.

## Harvey v Northumberland County Council [2003] EWCA Civ 338

H was employed by the Council as a residential social worker at a secure accommodation unit. The residents at the unit were disturbed children with behavioural problems who were likely to be volatile and aggressive.

There was an induction course for all staff when the unit opened, which covered the content of the Council's circular dealing broadly with restraint in Social Services establishments. Significantly, the circular gave no advice as to how employees should restrain individuals.

No further training had been given to staff at the time that H suffered an injury to his knee, while attempting to restrain a child who had become aggressive, though such a course was subsequently provided. H brought a claim for damages against the Council on the grounds that it had failed to provide adequate training in how to cope with children who needed to be restrained, in breach of its common law duty to ensure a safe workplace. The High Court judge found in favour of H and awarded him a total of £19,000 in damages.

The Council's appeal against that decision was dismissed by the Court of Appeal. The Court found that safer restraint techniques were available than those that were being used at the time of H's injury, and that while the Council knew that training was needed, it did not trouble to look and see where it might be found. The Council had a common law obligation to take reasonable steps to ensure the workplace was safe and it could not put that obligation on hold pending advice from official departments.

## Shot Guard Wins Right To Sue Firm

A Security Guard shot in an armed robbery seven years ago has won the right to claim compensation from his employers. Lord Justice Kennedy ruled that the risk of an armed attack in that area of Leeds had been "foreseeable", and that under *The 1992 Personal Protective Equipment at Work Regulations,* Securicor was obliged to make body armour available to its staff. A future compensation claim would be lawful. *(Reported in The Times, Saturday 18 May 2002.)*

**A girl who injured her back performing a headstand claimed £50,000 damages against her former school**

The girl was pressured into carrying out a high-risk exercise even though her teacher knew that she was hopeless at gymnastics. During the activity she fell backwards on the wooden floor and suffered a spinal injury. The girl's counsel claimed that his client had not had adequate instruction in how to carry out the headstand and the school had not carried out a proper risk assessment of the exercise. *(Reported in The Daily Telegraph, 26 February 2002.)*

This case shows the need to understand and make allocation for the physical ability of the staff being trained. Today very few physical skills courses are competently supervised.

Failure by an organisation to control the activity of self-defence/breakaway and/or physical restraint training and/or reduce the risks to its staff and others, including those individuals who may be the recipient of the use of force by organisational staff, leave the organisation open to claims for loss or injury suffered by those who either apply force or have force used on them.

## Codes of Practice—Buyer Beware!

There are certain codes of practice and guidance documents that are now being issued by various agencies regarding what employers and their staff can and cannot do with regard to the use of physical force. These 'codes of practice' provide guidance for commissioners of training and training providers on "best interest criteria".

Although many of these documents are well-intentioned many are written in line with a social policy for the minimisation of force as their core principle. Obviously the aim of these documents are to reduce the risk of injury to the vulnerable client group that staff are working with, however, although their value base may be laudable and credible from a social care perspective they could be promoting guidance which will actually increase the risk to staff and as such the liability of the organisation.

Another issue to consider here is if such professional bodies are going to promote advice on the use of physical force are they going to accept responsibility for it if an injury is sustained by an individual employee whose company has adhered to a particular Code of Practice?

A recent case that raises this issue is the case of the Welsh rugby player who has won his High Court case against the Welsh Rugby Union who now have to accept responsibility for the injury to Richard Vowles whose back was broken when a scrum collapsed. The Judge, Mr Justice Morland, ruled that David Evans, who refereed the game, had failed in his duty of care towards the players.

The case hinged on the decision by Llanharan to substitute an injured loose-head prop forward with a flanker who was inexperienced in the front row.

Under the practice of amateur rugby union, Llanharan could have chosen to have non-contested scrums, in which the packs do not push against each other, for the rest of the match. Llanharan did not take that option and Mr Vowles, the hooker, claimed that this decision led to the scrum collapsing when not properly engaged, paralysing him for life.

The Judge said that the referee had abdicated his responsibility, leaving it to Llanharan to decide whether to play non-contested scrums. Nick Bitel, a lawyer and the Chairman for the British Association of Sport and Law, said that the judge had concluded that the referee should have overruled the decision of the players. Since 1995, the rules of rugby union have specified that teams should have uncontested scrums if any unqualified players were in either front row.

Nigel Hook, senior technical officer of the Central Council of Physical Recreation, which represents the national governing bodies, said: *"This is a landmark case which will cause all our members to look very carefully at their regulations and insurance policies. We will be alerting the national governing bodies to the consequence of this case."*

Therefore, if any professional body is aiming to set itself up to govern what physical techniques may and may not be used they may need to accept the direct line of fault should an injury occur by compliance to a code of practice.

A fact that you should be aware of is that most occupational physical skill accreditation schemes are not a recognised qualification in physical skill. It is merely a system of accreditation by association for those training providers who wish to adopt the code of practice of a particular agency.

Many accreditation providers are also not registered as or regulated by any awarding body mandated by Government but are merely a self-regulating and self-accrediting agency who strive to promote good practice in their chosen field.

According to one such agency that we have spoken to directly, their accreditation is not aimed at accrediting an individual's or an organisation's competency in physical restraint. They also do not themselves offer training in physical intervention/restraint and/or advise on the issue.

In spite of this however, many public authorities have been advised to adopt the code of Practice promoted by them so as to be seen to be working towards a common standard. They have also been advised to use only those training providers accredited by the same agency whose code of practice they have also adopted.

# Mark Dawes

The main benefit for the training provider is that accreditation (or association with the accrediting agency) provides business opportunity leverage from organisations who are (themselves advised) to *only use accredited* agencies/individuals to deliver training.

The drawback for commissioning agencies (local authorities etc), if they follow this tack, is that they will engage the services of individuals and training providers whom they believe are accredited to a competent standard when actually they will be engaging the services of someone who is not actually officially accredited and who has not actually been assessed on their professional coaching competence but solely on compliance with whether or not their training complies with a code of practice.

As far as we are aware none of the accreditation panel for one such agency hold any nationally recognised coaching qualifications, are formerly health and safety qualified or have undertaken any in-depth legal training.

The reality of the situation is that such accreditation will not protect the commissioning agency, or indeed the training provider, from any liability that arises out of the negligence during training or in a claim for damages that may result from harm incurred during a restraint. In short the employer (the commissioning agency) will still have to show due diligence in their approach towards their selection of training provider.

111

# Understanding Reasonable Force

What this means is that risk assessments and 'training needs analysis' must be in place, and if some believe that by adopting 'accredited' agencies in absence of a suitable and sufficient risk assessment they will be protected they have been greatly deceived and should remember that a legal duty under *sections 2 and 3* of *The Health and Safety at Work Act* cannot be passed on by means of a contract.

# Mark Dawes

# Understanding Reasonable Force

# Endnote

Well, if you have reached this far you have done well. I hope you have enjoyed reading this book and that you have gained something from it.

It is my sincere hope that the language and examples used here have helped you gain a better understanding of what reasonable force is, or have at least moved you forward a few steps on your journey of knowledge in this area.

However, although this is the end of this book it may only be the beginning of your own personal journey in search of what it is that you hope to find that will increase the quality of your life or the quality of the lives of those that depend on you for your guidance, knowledge and experience.

The most important aspect that I believe a person can promote through their day-to-day activity is integrity. Without integrity a person shows by their deeds that they do not value that which they possess or give to others. Lack of integrity identifies itself as a lack of the understanding of a person's professional subject in a holistic way by the presentation of divided interests through a person's thoughts, words and deeds. To search for integrity allows a person to become one with themselves, and to give all of themselves for the benefit of others without conscious objection. To find integrity one must first seek the knowledge required to underpin one's own need for answers to questions that create a doorway for doubt to enter, or worse, the opinions of people that have no integrity.

*"Integrity without knowledge is weak and useless, and knowledge without integrity is dangerous and dreadful."*

—Samuel Johnson (1709 - 1784)

# Mark Dawes

# Understanding Reasonable Force

# References

- Andrew Ashworth, Principles of Criminal Law—Second Edition, Oxford University Press: 1997.
- John Wadham and Helen Mountfield, Blackstone's Guide to The Human Rights Act 1998, Blackstone Press Ltd: 2000.
- Expert Witness Basic Law Course Manual, September 2002
- Human Rights Task Force, The Human Rights Act: A New Era Of Rights And Responsibilities: Core Guidance For Public Authorities.
- NFPS Ltd.: Research Feedback & Private Correspondence.
- Officer Safety, Minimising the Risk of Violence: A Report by Her Majesty's Inspectorate of Constabulary—1997
- HSG65: Successful Health and Safety Management
- Health and Safety Executive, Health & Safety at Work Act etc 1974.
- HSG48: Reducing Error & Influencing Behaviour—Health and Safety Executive.
- Allan St John Holt, Safety for Senior Executives, IOSH Services: 1999.
- Management of Health and Safety at Work Regulations 1999, HSE Books.

Printed in the United Kingdom
by Lightning Source UK Ltd.
121480UK00001BA/283-309/A